The
SCRIBNER HOUSE
of NEW ALBANY

A Bicentennial Commemoration

ANNE CAUDILL, AMANDA DICK,
PAMELA PETERS *and* CARLENE PRICE

Enjoy this story of New Albany's Home Place.
— Anne F. Caudill

Charleston · Lon··
THE
History
PRESS

D1522854

Published by The History Press
Charleston, SC 29403
www.historypress.net

Cover image: C.W. Branham.

First published 2012

Manufactured in the United States

ISBN 978.1.60949.801.6

Library of Congress CIP data applied for.

Dedication

This account of Scribner House through two centuries is dedicated to
the women who have watched over and cared for it since 1814:

Mary Bull Scribner—wife of Joel Scribner, builder of the house
Caroline Chapman Scribner—first wife of William Augustus
Scribner, son of Joel and Mary
Harriet Partridge Scribner—second wife of William Augustus Scribner
Harriet Rowland Scribner ("Miss Hattie")—daughter of William
Augustus Scribner
Adaline von Moltwitz—housekeeper for the Scribner family for more
than six decades
and
to all those members of Piankeshaw Chapter of the National
Society Daughters of the American Revolution who, since 1917,
have struggled to preserve Scribner House as a memorial to the
founders of New Albany and as a living testimony to their influence.
They have made New Albany's homeplace available to its citizens
for study and pleasure.
Scribner House and the women of Scribner House are ready for
their third century.

By the River's Edge

Contents

Preface

M uch has been written about the pioneers who first ventured into the great forests and lands to the West, carrying their rifles, exploring the land to be settled by those who came after. The stories of how they brought their families and began the settlement of this land make a brave and fascinating saga.

But there came after them another kind of pioneer. These pioneers established the villages, towns and cities, bringing civic life to the new lands. They brought government, education, religion, commerce, banking and manufacturing. They, like the frontiersmen, risked much and undertook much. They had vision and courage.

With this second wave of pioneers came the Scribner family. Sons of a veteran of the Revolutionary War, they left the settled New England life of their forebearers, the pleasant towns, the churches and the schools, bringing wives and children to start anew in an unknown wilderness. They risked their lives and fortunes to build a new town on the far bank of the Ohio River in Indiana Territory.

The story of how Joel, Abner and Nathaniel Scribner founded the town of New Albany has been told and retold in many publications, all derived from court records and the accounts of family members preserved in the Indiana Room of the New Albany–Floyd County Public Library. This account seeks to tell the story of the Scribner House and the four generations of the Scribner family who made it their home for 103 years. The three brothers were only a part of the story of the influence that the Scribner family had

on the town they envisioned. On March 13, 1813, the first tree was felled
for construction of a log cabin—their first residence. Within three years,
their mother, Phebe Kellog Scribner, had joined her pioneering sons. Their
brother, James, and his sons, along with their sisters Esther, Elizabeth and
Phebe, with her husband, William Waring, and children had also arrived in
the new town. The difficulties of travel by wagon, carriage and flatboat to
reach the new settlement must have been formidable. Leaving the settled
towns of Long Island and New York City to start anew in log cabins with none
of the amenities to which they were accustomed took courage, perseverance
and skill. They were educated and capable men and women who established
home, church and school here on the banks of the Ohio. Most of the women
found themselves widowed early, but they carried the influence of the family
through to later generations. One extraordinary influence of the Scribner
family that still remains in this community is a scholarship fund they set up
in the public school system to be awarded each year to a worthy student. In
fact, at the time of New Albany's 175th anniversary, members of the Scribner
family who attended the celebration donated a large sum of money to help
sustain the scholarship.

Scribner House, built by Joel Scribner in 1814, was the first frame house
built in New Albany, and it is the oldest structure remaining. Its second
century has been in the care of Piankeshaw Chapter of the National Society
of the Daughters of the American Revolution. Joel Scribner's granddaughter,
Harriet Rowland Scribner (hereinafter referred to as "Miss Hattie"), was
a member of the DAR and sold the house to the chapter in May 1917.
She remained in the house until her death on September 20, 1917. Most
of the family possessions passed to the care of the chapter. Members have
worked hard at preserving the house and its contents as it appeared when
the Scribner family lived there. Today it is a museum dedicated to the family
who founded the town. But it was built as a home for a large family and
sheltered three generations of children. It was the homeplace for the many
relatives and, for a long time, the focal point of both business and social life
in New Albany.

Much of the following story was taken from written accounts of family
members over three generations. The Scribners were well-educated leaders
whose words carry us back to those early times. Some gaps in the story have
been filled in by later research. The story of the second century is distilled
from the minutes of the DAR Chapter and the recollections of the oldest
members. They reveal the dedicated struggle of the women of the chapter
to maintain the house and its artifacts and to make it available so that the

Scribner House, oldest known photo, 1850. *Courtesy Piankeshaw Chapter DAR.*

people of the community may visit their "home place" to see where the vision all began. Through all its years, it has been full of vibrant life. Now, with the help of the people of New Albany, we must work to ensure that it remains so for generations to come.

We gratefully acknowledge the work that Victor Megenity, Curtis Peters and Larry E. Price have done in proofreading this book and offering helpful suggestions. Their interest in preserving history is appreciated very much. We also thank Katherine Harding Holwerk for her tireless effort in preparing the images for this book.

Anne Caudill, Librarian of Piankeshaw Chapter DAR, 2012

Chapter 1

William Augustus Scribner's Recollection of Early Days in New Albany

The following journal, written by Dr. William Augustus Scribner, son of Joel Scribner, leaves a remarkable legacy for us regarding the founding of New Albany, Indiana. It is even more remarkable that the journal still exists in its original form.[1] Dr. Scribner, born in 1800, was already an old man and in ill health when he began writing his journal in 1862, at the request of his daughter, Miss Hattie. She pleaded with him to record his early recollections of the founding of New Albany. After all, he was thirteen years old when his family came down the Ohio River on a flatboat and first set foot on this land. It is, of course, a testimony to his character and strong religious faith that, first and foremost, he wanted to make an accurate record of the establishment of First Presbyterian Church in New Albany. Because he worked on recording those facts initially, it meant that before his death in 1868, he was never able to finish journaling his own personal experiences.

Scribner's recollection of names, dates and events, as well as the steady penmanship with which he personally recorded them, is truly extraordinary. An example of his detailed recollection is that of surveyor John K. Graham. William writes that his father, Joel, hired John K. Graham to measure out the streets of New Albany and that he, as a young boy, "assisted him as a chain carrier." He remembers that Graham, upon being hired, moved with his family to a cabin located several hundred feet west of the Scribners' cabin at present-day East Sixth and Main Streets. Also remarkable is the fact that the very chain that Graham used to measure the streets of New Albany is in the possession of the Floyd County Historical Society and is on display in the society's museum. A descendant of John Graham gave the chain to the society.

Dr. Scribner's incomplete journal, of course, leaves us with questions. He, for example, hardly mentions the Scribner House that is the focus of so much of our attention today. He

Dr. William Augustus Scribner, by George Morrison.
Courtesy Piankeshaw Chapter DAR.

writes only about the log cabin "dog trot" that his father built to accommodate the family when they first arrived.

There are other questions that you, the reader, may want to ask. But as you move through this book, be amazed at what Dr. Scribner and others have remembered and recorded about the founding of our beloved City of New Albany. There is no doubt that Dr. Scribner intended to revisit his manuscript and tidy it into a polished essay. As has been mentioned, however, he felt a strong compulsion to be the one in the family to take up the task of producing an accurate history of the Presbyterian Church in New Albany because his family was so instrumental in the organization of the church. He finished his church history but joined "the church triumphant" before he could return to his personal narrative.

(Transcriber's Note: In transcribing Dr. Scribner's journal, the spelling, sentence structure and punctuation have been left as they appeared in his original handwriting. Otis Amanda Dick, transcriber.)

Early Days In New Albany
A Personal History
With A Short Sketch of the Settlement Of New Albany
By William Augustus Scribner, M.D.

New Albany Ind., April 3rd, 1862.
My dear Daughter
    In compliance with your oft repeated and urgent requests, I now take my place at the desk, to give You some account, not only of my own early history,

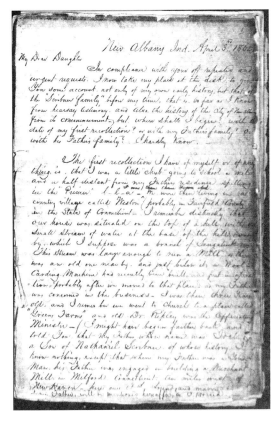

First page of Dr. William Augustus Scribner's diary.
Courtesy Indiana History Room, New Albany–Floyd County Public Library.

but that of the "Scribner family" before my time, that is, so far as I know from hearsay testimony, and also, the history of the City of New Albany from its commencement— but, where shall I begin? with the date of my first recollection? or with my Father's family? or with his Father's family? I hardly know.—

The first recollection I have of myself or of anything is, that I was a little "chub" going to school a mile and a half distant from my Father's residence, spelling in the "Primer," b-l-a. We were then living in a country village called Weston, (probably in Fairfield County) in the State of Connecticut—I remember distinctly that our house was situated on top of a hill, with a Small Stream of water at the base of the hill, running by which, I suppose, was a branch of Saugatuck River. This Stream was large enough to run a Mill, as there was an old one near by, and just below it, a Wool-Carding Machine had recently been built and put in operation, probably after we moved to that place, as my Father was concerned in the business—I was then three years old, and I remember we went to church to a place called "Green's Farms" and old Doctor Ripley was the Officiating Minister. (I might have begun farther back and told You, that my Father, whose name was Joel, was a son of Nathaniel Scribner, of whose history I know nothing, except that when my Father was a Young Man, his Father was engaged in building a Merchant Mill in Milford, Connecticut, ten miles west of New Haven here my Father found and married his wife. My Mother was the daughter of Jabez Benedict and Mara N(aomi) Bull, and her name was Mary—her mother used to call her "Polly." Our family, however, moved from Milford before my recollection, and perhaps to this same town of Weston.

My father, Joel Scribner, was born at South East, Duchess County, New York, in the year 1772.

Of my Grandfather Scribner I know but little, but have learned that he was a Captain in the Revolutionary War, and was wounded in the battle of (Monmouth) in the arm, by a musket ball, which entered at the wrist and came out at the elbow. After the close of the war, he with his family, moved from Duchess County to Compo in Connecticut, on Long Island Sound. Efforts have been made to ascertain to what company and regiment he belonged, in what engagements he fought, and where he was wounded, but the answer returned from the War Department in Washington, states that the records were destroyed by fire, and his name appears in the Pension Office as a Captain of Connecticut Volunteers, drawing a pension up to the time of his death, which occurred in the year 1800, in the town of Louisville, Georgia, whither he had gone on business. He was a man very much beloved by all who knew him, being generous and kind in his disposition, and was possessed of very ample means which became lost through speculation.

My first recollection of my Grandma Scribner, whose maiden name was Phebe Kellogg; is, when I was some four or five years old, that she was, at that time, to me, an elderly lady, living at Compo, Connecticut, with some two or three of her younger children, a woman of strong mind, great mathematical powers, and deep religious feeling.

My Grandparents on both Father's and Mother's sides, were blessed with a number of children, but my Mother's parents and relatives, all living in and around Milford, I never knew much concerning them, as we seldom saw any of them.

There were twelve children of the Scribner family, six of each sex living at the time we moved from New York in Oct. 1811, all but one of whom I have seen, and have been acquainted with the most of them. Their names were—Eliphalet,—James,—Jemima,—Joel,—Phebe and Martha (twins),— Esther,—Elijah,—Elizabeth,—Nathaniel,—Anna,—Abner. Perhaps I have not named them according to their ages, but I have, as well as I can recollect. I have nothing but memory for my guide.

Eliphalet went to the West Indies before or about the time that I was born, say in the year 1800, and died there some twenty or twenty-five years after.

Jemima became the wife of Mr. Samuel Penny and lived in Bridgeport, Connecticut, for a few years, whence they removed to New York City, where Mr. and Mrs. Penny died.

Martha (we used to call her Aunt Patty) became the wife of Uriah Rogers Scribner, her own cousin. I remember distinctly the time she was married. Her mother was living at a place called Compo, in Connecticut, on Long Island Sound, which was about three miles from Saugatuck, where my Father then lived, and I, some four or five years old, was at the wedding.

James married and lived in the State of New York, some fifty or sixty miles above the City, and soon after New Albany was laid out, immigrated to this place, being then a widower with two sons, Alanson and Isaac.

Phebe married a Mr. William Waring and settled in Ridgefield, Connecticut. The other brothers and sisters of my Father will be mentioned hereafter, as I proceed.

My parents have told me that I was born on the 19th day of Feby 1800, in the aforesaid town of Milford, and my Brother Harvey; the firstborn, on the 3rd day of August 1798—next was my Sister, Lucy Maria; next—Mary Lucinda—I cannot now call to mind the time of their births, nor the place where we lived at the time, but my impression is, that it was at "Weston." Eliphalet being next, I remember distinctly, was born at Saugatuck, and I think it was in January 1806. Sister Julia Ann was next, and we then lived about 3 miles from Norwalk (Ct) at a place called "Shercrow," which I believe is an Indian name, and near to an Uncle of my Father's whose name was Enoch Scribner. I think this was in April 1807, and I remember distinctly that Brother Harvey and I had the Meazles at the time of her birth, and that we were prohibited from seeing the precious "baby" for a long time as we then thought, and I think it probable the other children might have had the disease at the same time, but I do not know or remember for certain—

In the Fall of 1807, I was sent to Stamford, another town in Connecticut, near the Long Island Sound, say 50 miles from New York where my Grandmother Scribner then lived—I remained with them all that Winter and went to school—sometimes in the snow over knee-deep—Some two or three of my unmarried Aunts were at home with their Mother—I remember distinctly Aunts Esther and Anna, and I think a part of the time, Elizabeth, though Aunt Elizabeth might have come home on a visit, as I remember that she was at a Boarding-School in New Jersey, finishing up her education.

In the early part of the year 1808, my Father moved to the City of New York, and soon afterwards perhaps in March or April, my Grandmother & family moved to Morristown, New Jersey, some 30 miles from New York—

but we went to New York first, and I remained at my Father's, who was then living on the corner of Broadway & Spring St. in a new two Story Brick House, the front being used as a "Family Grocery" and "Feed Store" of which my Father was the proprietor—

During the latter part of the Spring of 1808 or 1809 (I cannot remember which) I was put on board a Small Sloop, under the care of Captn Bristol, a cousin of my Mother's and was handed over by him early on the morning of the following day, to my relatives in the aforesaid town of Milford—The Captn left me at the house of Mr Wm Atwater, whose wife was the only Sister of my Mother. I remained there, perhaps a couple of hours, when one of my Cousins came in, a Son of my Mother's Brother, and escorted me up to the old homestead, and introduced me to my Grandfather & Grandmother Bull. The old lady was in the Pantry, when I first entered the house, which was a small room, the floor of which was a foot or two below the level of the other rooms—We (my Cousin & myself) had gone into the front door without knocking and were standing in the middle of the floor, when Grandma came stepping up out of the Pantry, and appeared as if she was about to meet some strangers, but I noticed she made a straight line towards me, first looking at me through her Spectacles, of which she had two pair on her head, then, lowering her head and peering over the glasses, having by this time come close up to me, threw up her arms and exclaimed in a loud voice, "I do believe this is one of Polly Bull's children!" and then she gathered me and wanted to know how I came there &c. &c. from all of which I suppose she must have been taken by surprise—

There were several Brothers of my Mother's residing in Milford, who had families, some of the Cousins being older and some younger than myself—A few days after my arrival I began to go to school—as I remember in a Small Brick House I think it was, in the centre of a large Square—I made my home chiefly at Grandpa's, spending, now and then, a few days at the house of some uncle, where I invariably found "lots" of children (cousins)—And of course, during my stay, I became quite well acquainted with many of my Mother's Kin. Before I left, I assisted Grandpa in digging his potatoes, and I well remember that we found one very large; which pleased the old Gentleman very much, so that he took it to one of the Stores and weighed it, and my impression is, that its weight was 2 $\frac{3}{4}^{lbs}$. I returned to New York in the month of October on the same vessel, Capt. Bristol, and had a pleasant voyage—

On the 1st day of April 1810, I was sent to Morristown, New Jersey, I think my Father accompanied me. The ride was twenty-eight miles by stage, after crossing the ferry at the foot of Courtland Street. I found my Grandmother, (my Father's Mother) living there with three of her daughters, (viz) Esther, Elizabeth, and Anna—conducting a Female Boarding School & House Keeping. I boarded with them and attended the Academy for boys, which was quite a celebrated School in those days—it was a large, two story, Frame Building—with two large rooms in each story, besides the basement—Three Brothers by the name of Whelpley were the Teachers—Wm Whelpley taught the languages, James Whelpley, the higher branches in English, he was my teacher—and Orlando, the youngest Brother, the Primary department in the basement—After remaining One Year, I went home during vacation, and returned in about a week, and stayed until the Fall of 1811—

During my absence in 1810, my sister Phebe was born.

My Father having determined to emigrate to the West, he formed a Partnership with his Brother-in-law, Wm. Waring, (he Waring) being a practical Tanner & Currier, to establish themselves in business in Cincinnati, Ohio—Accordingly on the 8th day of October, 1811, the two families left New York City in a small vessel, & crossing New York Bay, 15 miles, landed in New Jersey at Elizabethtown—We had a wagon for each family, each drawn by three horses—One of the horses met with an accident in getting out of the Boat at Elizabethtown, hurting one of his legs quite seriously, on which account we were compelled to remain for several days—this was considered one of the best and strongest horses of the whole six, and although we were then on expenses, our men-folks thought it best and most economical to wait, and let him get entirely well before leaving—So on the 17th day of Oct having been detained 8 or 9 days almost in sight of the home we had left, we took up our line of March for the "Far-West"—which indeed it was in those early times—Our whole company consisted of William Waring & wife, and his Brother Harry Waring (unmarried), & four children, (to-wit,) Jesse—Nathaniel—Moses—and George; the oldest perhaps, not more than seven or eight years—these all belonged to what we called our "Yankee Wagon"—then Joel Scribner & wife, with their children, Harvey—Wm Augustus—Lucy Maria—Mary Lucinda—Eliphalet—Julia Ann—and Phebe, Seven occupying our "Jersey Wagon", making a total of 5 adult persons and 11 children—We journeyed directly across the State of New Jersey, passing through Scotch Plains, Plainfield, Somerville, and many other towns, the names of which I do not remember; crossing the River Delaware at Easton, and travelled through the State of Pennsylvania to Pittsburgh, on what was, at that time, considered to be the best route—A great many towns, no doubt, have been laid out and built up since that time, and many that we passed through, I have forgotten—but I will give you the names of some of the principal ones—Leaving Easton, then, we passed through Bethlehem, Allentown, crossing the River "Schuylkill" at Reading, and the "Susquehanna" at Harrisburgh, the Capital of the State, then journeying through Carlisle, Shippensburgh, Chambersburgh, Bedford, Somerset, Laurel Hill, and Greensburgh, to Pittsburgh.—many incidents occurred on our journey, but being compelled to give you this little history entirely from memory, not having even the scratch of a pen for reference, and so many years having elapsed since, I shall not be able to give you many of the particulars, only now and then <u>one</u>, which made a distinct impression on my mind at the time.—

In the first place, then, There was a difference of opinion between the Messrs Warings, and my Father, as to the propriety of travelling on Sunday— the Warings in favor of it, as, in their opinion, we could keep the Sabbath as well in that way as to stop, gaining time and lessening expenses—but my Father, on the contrary, being a Christian Man, objected, argueing not only the great sin of Sabbath-breaking, but insisted that by resting, our horses would stand the journey better, as well as men, women, and children, and he verily believed we should gain time instead of losing it, and so it was, we rested on Sunday—I remember that we tarried some two or three days at Reading, perhaps having to make some repairs to our wagons, horse-shoeing, &c, &c.

We arrived at Carlisle just before sunset, intending to put up for the night, but the Court being in Session, we were told by all the tavern-keepers that they were full and we could not be accommodated, so we drove on three miles and stopped at a country tavern—and such fare as we had! Uncle Waring & myself took one of our horses, hitched him before a sled with a Barrel on it, and went about two miles to get it filled with water, so that we might have a <u>little</u> for ourselves and horses, and besides that, we could get nothing of the grain kind but green corn to feed our horses, the consequence of which was, that the next day one of our horses became sick and died at Shippensburgh—then we (that is, the children) thought we were almost broke up—however, we journeyed westward, and the next day met a Man with an old revolutionary-looking steed and bought him for Fifteen Dollars—The roads, nearly all the way, were exceedingly muddy and our progress necessarily slow, & what made them still worse, turnpikers were at work ploughing up the old road in many places, so that we found it very hard work to get through—we met with many large <u>road-wagons</u>, drawn by 5 & 6 horses, hauling goods across the Mountains to Pittsburgh for western merchants, there being no other mode of transportation at that time—We made it convenient to reach the top of the Allegany Mountain about sun down, though we could not see the sun, as it was raining, and put up at a large Stone Tavern, finding many travellers and some teamsters in before us—we called for supper, but it seemed as if we should all starve before it was ready, and after waiting till about 9 o'clock, we had some hot coffee, fried chicken, and other good "fixins" which were not bad to take.—

The next morning just as we had harnessed up, ready for a start, two men came riding up briskly, saying that some one had stolen some Shovels or Pick Axes, and they pretended to have a Search Warrant—and said something about Searching our wagons, & c. My Father told them to search his and welcome, but they did not seem inclined to do it. Uncle Waring on the contrary, took his heavy wagon whip in his hand, and standing near his wagon, being very indignant, swore by his Maker that the first man who made the least attempt to search his wagon, would be knocked down—that they might know, that movers, as we were, had enough to haul through the mud, without any of their Shovels or Picks; and furthermore, doubted whether they had any thing in the shape of a Search-Warrant, and was more likely after stealing something themselves: the result of all which was, that they kept themselves at a respectful distance, making no effort to search his wagon—

We reached Pittsburgh as near as I can recollect, about the 1st November, all very much rejoiced that we had done travelling through the mud—After resting a few days, we purchased a small Flat-Boat say 50 feet long, by 12 or 13 wide, and fitting it up as conveniently as we could, for the women and children, and getting some provisions aboard and all our plunder; except the horses, which we sent through by land—we weighed anchor, and started for Cincinnati, taking it very moderately, and tying up at night, the River being very low, arrived at Cincinnati on the 30th day of November, being just 3 weeks since we left Pittsburgh—we found it extremely difficult to procure a house, so many imigrants arriving daily & we had to remain in the Boat at the shore, for five weeks, which brought us into the first week in January before we left it—Many other families in Boats along shore went through the same ordeal—

Uncle Waring obtained a house on or near Water Street in the upper part of the town and moved his family into it. The house we first moved into, was a small frame, on one of the back streets, which we occupied but a short time, & then moved into a new two story brick immediately in the rear of an old frame, situated on the west side of Main Street at the top of the hill or second rise, owned by a Mr Ezekiel Hall, a Boot & Shoe Maker, & who carried on his business in an adjoining building—

Flatboat such as the Scribners would have used. *Courtesy Indiana History Room, New Albany–Floyd County Public Library.*

It was the purpose of Scribner & Waring, immediately upon our arrival at Cincinnati, to establish themselves in the Tanning business on a large and extensive scale, & they very soon began to purchase <u>hides</u> for that purpose, before they had even selected a site for a Tan Yard—It was their intention also to add to their business, the Boot & Shoe making in all its various branches—Mr Harry Waring superintending that department, & in a short time they had a large Shoe Shop in operation—In order to compete with the best shops of the kind in the place, & for the purpose of procuring the very best material for "fine work", it was thought best that my Father should visit New York and purchase such Stock as they desired—Accordingly, he left his family, strangers as we were in a strange place, & as there was nothing better than Stage Coaches in those days, for the travelling public, he was gone nearly all winter and had the misfortune of having his pocket picked of $300 in Bank Bills, on his return, soon after leaving New York, perhaps at New Brunswick in New Jersey—which was one cause of his long absence—When he discovered that his pocket had been cut open, and no Pocket Book in it, (it was about midnight) he called for a light, the stage having just then driven up to a Stage House, & found his Pocket Book lying wide open in the bottom of the Stage & the papers it had contained lying around loose, but the Money was all gone—He used every means to try to find it, by causing his fellow passengers to be searched, and one suspicious looking fellow, whose place in the stage was immediately behind him, he had searched some two or three times, in different places, but never a Five Dollar Bill did he find of it—This, under the circumstances, was a very sad catastrophe—

During this winter, I think in the month of Feby (1812) the whole Western Country was visited with Earthquakes, many of which were very severe, so much so, that in Cincinnati, the inhabitants were very much alarmed, and some almost terror-stricken, forsaking their houses for the street, for the time being, and the Town of New Madrid in the State of Missouri on the Mississippi River was almost destroyed by them—

According to the custom in those days, all the men between the ages of 18 and 45, had to train or muster as it was called, either among the militia of the State or in some independent or volunteer company—The two Mr Warings concluded that they could not condescend to appear among the militia so Wm Waring joined a Cavalry Company & was made an Officer of his company (& a finer looking officer on horse-back would be hard to find)—Harry joined a Light Infantry Company, & soon after which, War was declared between the United States and England, commonly called the War of 1812; and when a call was made for soldiers to go to the frontier, to Detroit, for instance, these two companies in which were the Mr. Warings, were among the first to be offered, who, of course, were received; and this was the cause of the breaking up of all the business arrangements of the firm of Scribner and Waring. Consequently the stock on hand of hides, leather and manufactured work had to be sold off to the best advantage, and during the summer and fall of this year, my Father remaining at home, closed up the business of the concern. Martha Ann Waring was born March 17th, 1812 in Cincinnati, Ohio. During this year, all the troops from Kentucky, Tennesee, and Indiana, passed through Cincinnati on their way north, which was a very interesting spectacle, especially for the children, who seemed to enjoy it very much.

Cincinnati was a small town when we first arrived, though it was filling up with immigrants chiefly from the north and east. At the time there were no public improvements of any kind, except a small Market House on the bottom just east of Main Street, perhaps. No street improvements, no wharf or other improvement of the bank of the river. There was an old stone building called the Court house standing on the hill west of Main street, near and a little north of Doctor Wilson's old frame church, with a large graveyard in the rear, west of it.

During the fall of 1812, My Father's brothers, Nathaniel and Abner Scribner, came to Cincinnati, and in December or January following, they, with my Father, started off on an exploring expedition, and after viewing the present site of New Albany and the country for a short distance around, concluded to make the purchase of the tract of land upon which the city is located, having in view, before the purchase, the idea of laying out a part of it into Town-lots. Upon inquiry they ascertained the owner of the land to be Col. John Paul, a resident at that time, of Madison, Indiana. They went immediately to see him and made a purchase of all his ownership of land lying in Fractional Sections N°s 2 and 3—together with the sole right of ferriage across the Ohio river from said Fractional Sections of land—And very soon after their return to Cincinnati, we began to make our arrangements for leaving Ohio for Indiana—On the 2nd day of March, 1813, the first tree was cut down, by way of beginning to clear a spot for a Cabin to be placed for a dwelling house. This particular spot was just above what is now Capt. Samuel Montgomery's present residence, on the same side of Main Street. On the 2nd day of May, just two months from the date of the first cutting, the two families before mentioned, to-wit, my Father's and William Waring's landed at the place we now call the Upper Ferry landing, and found this dwelling house of two months in building, to be a large "double cabin" with quite a wide hall between them and a large kitchen attached to one of the wings, as yet in an unfinished state, and although made of green logs, just from the woods, we, of course, were compelled to occupy them in the condition they were and make the best of it, and finish them up during the summer—Of course you will expect to be told that at that time, the place where the City of New Albany now stands, was a perfect wilderness, and it was, indeed. Not only very heavily timbered with Poplar, Beech, & Sugar Trees, the usual production of the river bottoms, but the whole surface of the earth was thickly covered with Spicewood, Pawpaw, Greenbrier, and almost every other growth incident to a rich soil—really, it was so thick in the Spring & Summer, after the leaves had obtained their full growth, that one could not see more than a rod ahead, in the woods. Oh! it was romantic, especially on the top of Cane Knob, west of the City—where we could take a fine view of the surrounding country—

Well, the first thing to be done was to procure a Surveyor, and commence the survey and Platting of the Town—and I can hardly tell you, how or where the Proprietors found the one who had the honor of doing it—his name was John K. Graham & my first recollection of him is that he moved his family into a small cabin built after we came here, located some two or three hundred Yards this side and west of ours, and I soon became acquainted with him, as I often assisted him as chain carrier—After some time he bought a

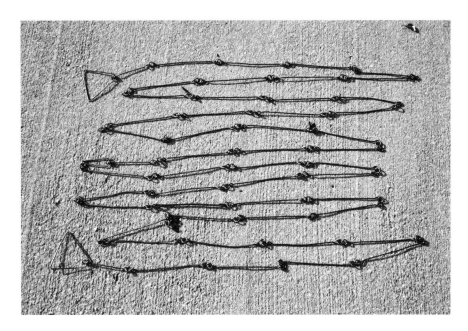

Chain used by John K. Graham to measure the streets of New Albany. *Courtesy Floyd County Historical Society. Photo by Curt Peters.*

farm or rather a tract of land, some three or four miles north and moved to it. During all the summer of 1813, we had a number of men hired to work at chopping down trees and piling the brush, building cabins, grubbing the undergrowth, and more especially, where streets were known to run, and the Proprietors commenced very soon the building of a Steam Saw Mill, and did afterward connect a Grist Mill with it—this was built on the Ground where the Foundry of Lent South & Shipman now stands—Among other buildings, one among the first after the family residence, was a large, square Cabin for a School House, on one of four Public Squares, on each side of the intersection of State and Spring Streets, not far from where the Court House now stands, which said building was also occupied frequently for a Meeting House, until we could build a larger one—

The first Public-Sale of lots in the <u>Town of New Albany</u>, took place on the 2nd & 3rd days of November 1813—by which time, there were several log cabin residences, along down Main Street from the one we occupied, reaching as far down perhaps as Lower 2nd Street, and in the course of the summer, quite a number of families had moved in—

We pass over to the summer of 1815—My Sister Harriet was born in New Albany Feby or March 1815. In the month of June of this Year, Uncle

Nathaniel Scribner was under necessity of going to New York on business, and I accompanied him to Cincinnati—this, you will observe, was before any Steam Boats were running on the River, or any other public conveyance for travellers; so we left here on horseback, travelling through Kentucky, and passing by "Big Bone Lick" we performed the journey in three days—I found Cincinnati looking pretty much as we had left it two years before, except that the City authorities had begun to improve their streets somewhat by grading & paving, and building a wharf at the foot of Main Street, and I remember, too, that Doctor Wilson's old frame church building had been demolished, and a substantial brick one was in course of erection, on or near the same ground. I remained there some three weeks, and before I left, the first story window frames had been put in their places; while there, Uncle Nath¹ made a horse trade with a man of his acquaintance, by which he got two for one, the consequence of which was, that I had a horse to lead home besides the one I rode—but as well as I can remember, I got along very well on the journey home, consuming three days as before—I was then 15 Years of age—Uncle Nathaniel returned in the Fall, and his Sister Esther & the present Aunt Clapp (who was then Miss Elizabeth Edmonds) came out with him, and soon afterwards Uncle Nath¹ & Miss Edmonds were married—I do not now recollect at what time Uncle James Scribner came west, neither the precise time that Grandma & Aunt Elizabeth arrived, but they were all here within two or three years of our first landing here—

In the summer of 1816, I went to live as a Store Boy with one James Pearson at Paoli, Orange County, Indiana, and remained with him 8 months, came home the latter part of April, and about the 1ˢᵗ of June, I went to Vincennes into the Drug Store of Messʳˢ Hale & Wood—Doct Hale some time previous had become the husband of Aunt Esther, and perhaps in 1818 Mr. Wood married Aunt Elizabeth—I returned from Vincennes in October 1817, and found nothing special at home for me to do, my Father at that time not being engaged in any business which required my services— He was elected Clerk and Recorder of the County of Floyd, soon after the County was formed, which I think, was the following winter.

During the session of the Legislature of 1818 & 19, Uncle Nathaniel and our Surveyor Jn. K. Graham went to Corydon, the seat of Government at that time, to use all their influence with the members to grant our petition for a new County, we were then in Clark County—The Legislature granted the petition at that session—Uncle Nathl was taken sick while at Corydon, and on his way home, became worse—he parted with Mʳ Graham on the top of the Knob near where the town of Edwardsville now stands, and after getting down the Knob and almost home, he was compelled to stop at a house on the road, becoming too sick to travel further—Mʳ Richard Watson was the occupant of the house, some 2 ½ miles from here, on the Corydon road—Uncle N. remained there all night and while we were eating breakfast the next morning, a messenger came for the Doctor, informing us that he was very sick—Doct. Clapp was then boarding at my Father's, and he and my Father & Uncle James Scribner, started immediately for Mr. Watsons, and found the patient past all hope of recovery—he died during the day, or that night. This was in the latter part of December 1818, and the weather was bitter cold—

Note—My sister Mary was married to Dr. Asahel Clapp (I think) in the summer of 1819, and died the latter part of August, as near as I can remember in 1821, within a day or two, after having given birth to a little dear immortal (Aug 30. 1821).

William Scribner Clapp died Oct 8, 1821, aged 5 weeks, 4 days

Asahel Clapp and Mary Lucinda Scribner were married at New Albany, September 30, 1819

Asahel Clapp & Elizabeth Edmonds Scribner were married at New Albany, Jan. 31 1822

Nathaniel Scribner died Dec 14, 1818 aged 35 years.

In the month of March 1818, I commenced the Study of Medicine with Doct. Clapp, and continued with him until August, 1822, when, after being examined by the Medical Society, in June, at Charlestown, Clark County, I went to the aforesaid Town of Paoli and commenced the Practice of Medicine. I very soon formed the acquaintance of a Merchant by the name of Thomas F. Chapman, an Eastern Man, from Hanover, New Hampshire, who was very successful in his business, and in the year 1826, he loaded a couple of Flat Boats with Produce, Flour, Beef, & Pork, at Leavenworth on the Ohio, 26 miles South of Paoli, and started to New Orleans for a Market, but was, unfortunately, taken sick, and died before he reached there; being buried at a place called the "Red Church," some 20 miles above the city—It was his intention, immediately after his return, to visit Hanover, his old home, and bring out with him his two sisters, they being the only near relatives he had living, his Mother having died, I think, in the year 1823 or 24—and You must know that he had promised me his Youngest sister for a wife—Of course that was jesting in earnest—The news of his death was received at Paoli, on the 4ᵗʰ day of July 1826, & such a distressed wife and children (of whom there were four) I hardly ever witnessed—Being the family Physician, I was very intimate at the house and treated already like a Brother—and

An original image of Dr. William Augustus Scribner as an older man. Artist unknown. *Photo by C.W. Branham.*

it became my painful duty to write to the sisters conveying the melancholy intelligence of his death— They being aware of his intended visit in the Fall, concluded, after his death, that it was a duty they owed to him and his family, to make a visit to them, as there was nothing special to Keep them at Hanover— They accordingly made arrangements for the journey, and started late in the fall or early in the winter of 1827, for Paoli and after travelling as far as Cincinnati, the weather becoming very cold, the River froze up & they could proceed no further except by land, and there being no public conveyance, they remained there some weeks—Mrs Chapman, the widow, feeling very anxious about them, having received several letters from them while at Cincinnati, was much concerned to know how to get them to Paoli—

Providentially, a four horse Spring Waggon put up one night at the Public House opposite to Mrs Chapman's residence, filled with Members of Congress, & would go as far as Cincinnati with them, and return empty unless passengers could be found coming west—So Mrs Chapman called on me to write to the girls, by the driver of this conveyance, (who, by the way, was quite a Gentleman) and make up their minds to take passage with him for Paoli, and they did even so—and during the succeeding Fall, to-wit, on the 25th day of October, 1827, Miss Caroline Matilda Chapman, changed her name for Mrs Doct. Scribner—I might have mentioned before that during the summer, the said Caroline taught school at Paoli for some six months—

Harvey Kellogg Scribner, our first born, was born at Paoli, Orange County, Indiana, Sept. 16th, 1828, and died Oct. 5th living 19 days.—

Harvey Augustus Scribner, born at Paoli, Nov. 28th 1829.

We lived in Paoli after our marriage until January 1831—when I sold out my little property, and moved to New Albany, and became a Partner in business with Doct. Clapp.

During my residence at Paoli, Uncle James Scribner died I think in the summer of 1823—his wife and Son Alanson, also died while I lived there—his son Isaac, went to St. Francisville, La. and died there some time in 1822 I think—

My Father died in October, 1823 of Bilious Fever—and my Brother Eliphalet, followed him in January 1824 of Congestion of the Brain—he would have been 18 years old, had he lived a few days longer—

Uncle Abner died at Memphis Tenn. in the latter part of the summer or Fall of 1827—& Grandma Scribner in September of the same year—aged about 80 years—

New Albany, February 8th 1867.

Nearly five years since as you will perceive by the date, I wrote the foregoing narrative, except that I have now added some few Notes and interlineations by way of correcting in some particulars, and in others, to be more explicit—

We will now take a long step backwards, and consider ourselves just entered upon the year 1816. And the first subject I take up will be the organization of the First Presbyterian Church, in which our family took so prominent a part; and in order to give you the full particulars, I here copy from the Church Records of that date, which is of course authentic:

"RECORD"

"On the 16th day of February A.D. 1816, a church was organized at Jeffersonville, in the state of Indiana, composed of Members residing in that place and New Albany, by the Rev[d]. James McGready, a Missionary under a Commission from the General Assembly, which church was to be known by the name of the Union Church of Jeffersonville and New Albany—The Sacrament of the Lord's Supper was, at that time administered, and the following were the members then in communion; viz:—Thomas Posey, (then Gov[r]) & his wife, John Gibson & his wife, James M. Tunstal, James Scribner (my Uncle), Joel Scribner (my Father), Phebe Scribner (my Grandmother), Esther Scribner (my Aunt & afterwards Mrs.

Hale) and Anna M. Gibson; of whom Thomas Posey and Joel Scribner were chosen Elders."—

"Subsequent to that time, Mary Merriwether, the wife of Doct' Merriwether, and Mary Wilson, a widow, were received as Members of the said Church.—Since that time, Thomas Posey and his wife, removed to Vincennes and united with the Church at that place; John Gibson and his wife removed to Pittsburgh, and united with the Church there; and James Tunstal went to Louisville and joined the Church there; and Mary Merriwether, Mary Wilson, and Anna M. Gibson, were at their requests, dismissed from this Church to join the church in Louisville."

"Afterward, to wit, on the 7ᵗʰ day of December A.D. 1817, at a Meeting of the Members of the Union Church at New Albany, the Revᵈ D.C. Banks, Moderator, It was Resolved, That as all the members of this Church, residing at Jeffersonville, have withdrawn, and all the present Members reside in New Albany; the Union Church shall, from this time, hereafter be Known by the Name of The First Presbyterian Church of New Albany. At the same time, Jacob Marsell and Hannah his wife were received as Members of this Church, on a letter from the Church in Elizabethtown, New Jersey; Stephen Beers and Lydia his wife, were also received as Members of this Church, on a letter from the Church in Louisville, Ky."

"The Church then proceeded, by ballot, to the election of two additional Elders; Jacob Marsell and Stephen Beers were unanimously elected, and accordingly were afterwards ordained as ruling Elders in this Church. Members in communion at the close of the year 1817-9 "

The Meeting of the Church at the time of its organization took place in Grandma Scribner's house, being what is now the middle part of the old "High Street House;" the Congregation occupying the Parlor and back room. There being no communion plate, two large Pewter Plates belonging to my Grandmother were used instead, for the bread, and being of a very fine quality were considered even very appropriate.

The next year, 1818, we had the ministerial labors of the Revᵈ Isaac Reed, from, perhaps, the latter part of the summer for One Year ensuing. After he left us the Church was vacant for some time. At the end of the year 1818, the number of Church Members was 17, and at the end of the year 1819, they had increased to 32. I perceive by reference to the Records of the Church, that my Sister Lucy Maria, with myself and several others united with the church on the 31ˢᵗ day of October of this year (1819); that Aunt Clapp (then Widow Elizabeth Scribner) on the 4ᵗʰ day of September of the same year, at the same time her infant daughter Lucinda Anna, (now Mrs. Shipman) was baptized; and that Cousin Martha Ann Waring (now Mrs. Gonzales) was also baptized on the 28th of November following.

Miss Hattie added the following note to her father's journal:

And here my Father's record ends, much to my grief and disappointment. During the fall of 1867 I brought him my book urging him to finish the Record as I was so anxious about it. His reply was: "Leave it right here on my table, & as I have leisure I will write in it." I left it—but at the time my Father was very much engaged in making a new Church Record, taking it from the beginning up to that time, making a more explicit and plainer one than the old one and placing it all in one large book. He was not well much of the time while he was engaged in the work, and my Mother urged him very much one day to desist, telling him he would feel worse for it. His answer was: "My Dear, I must finish this work. No one living can do it as I can, and I want to leave a clean Record behind me." And a clean Record he did leave. Twas beautiful to look at. Everything separated, the one from the other: All the organizations of Church, Sunday School, Ordination of Ministers, Elders, Deacons, and members of the church; dates concerning everything, baptized children, etc., from the beginning up to that time. The only thing that was not entirely complete was the list of baptized children, a few names that he had never been able to get from the late former Pastor of the church, were not recorded.

Knowing that he was not at all well, I did not like to urge him much to write in 'my book,' as I called it, but I ventured one day to say, "Father, please write some in my book. I am afraid I shall not get any more done." He replied: "Just wait till I get this done and I'll write in yours everyday till I finish it, but this work must be done."

But Alas for human calculation. As soon as the church Record was finished, the Master thought his work was done and He called him from the "Church Militant to the Church Triumphant."

And so, we move from the journal of Dr. William Augustus Scribner to the next chapter, where we learn more from several other sources: obituaries, census records, newspaper articles, correspondence and accounts written by a family member.

Chapter 2

More About the Scribners, Their Neighbors and Kin

In 1863, fifty years after the Scribners first arrived at the site of New Albany, the *New Albany Daily Ledger* interviewed Dr. William Augustus Scribner and published his recollection of that early time. He recounted the following:

> *The rude boat landed at the same spot where the ferry boats now land at the foot of Upper (East) Fifth Street. There were occupied cabins in the place on each side of the ferry landing (Nicholsons and Truebloods). The first ground cleared was on the south side of what is now Main Street, between Pearl and Bank on which four cabins were built, the contract for which was taken by a Mr. Wright for $25.00 each. The floors were made of puncheons (half logs laid cut side up), the chimneys three cornered, and the openings between the logs chinked and daubed. The surface of the new town presented a very uninviting appearance. The timber was very heavy, the undergrowth very thick, and the ground terribly uneven. Numerous ravines extended through its entire length and breadth.*[2]

In 1868, Dr. William Augustus Scribner died, and except for the above interview and his journal, his record of early New Albany and the Scribners' family life remained incomplete. His daughter, Miss Hattie, wrote of his unfinished work and planned to continue it. However, from Miss Hattie we have only some genealogical information about earlier and collateral branches of the Scribner family that she obtained. Many years later, she was interviewed twice about the family by the local newspapers. Her niece, Mary Helen Scribner, daughter of Miss Hattie's brother, Harvey, wrote two accounts of life in the Scribner House that are reproduced in the next two chapters. Born in New Albany in 1879, Mary Helen was, from infancy, a constant visitor at the Scribner House. It is from her two accounts, therefore, that we have an intimate picture of the house and the personalities who lived within its walls.

Researching the archives of the Indiana Room of the New Albany–Floyd County Public Library has also brought to light information that Dr. Scribner did not record.

EARLY DEVELOPMENT OF NEW ALBANY

The first plat of New Albany was recorded November 13, 1816. The plat shows that Water Street was one hundred feet wide and extended along the Ohio River. The original Water Street disappeared with the building of the flood wall; however, present-day Water Street basically replicates the original thoroughfare. The next parallel street was High Street (now Main) and was eighty feet wide. Following were Market and Spring Streets, also eighty feet wide. The parallel streets north of there began to narrow, with Elm being sixty feet wide and Oak just thirty feet wide.

Regarding the streets running north and south, State Street became the center of the new town, with all numbered streets above it being called Upper First, Upper Second and so on and all streets below State being designated Lower First, etc. It is obvious from the description of the first streets that Joel Scribner built his house right in the center of activity. The Scribner brothers surely had a hand in assisting surveyor Graham with the work of naming these first streets. They also had the forethought of designating platted areas for churches, schools, municipal areas and a park. The fact that education was important to them can be seen in the fact that they set up an endowment for the education of New Albany's children. The fund is still in existence and each year provides a scholarship for a worthy student. The fund is managed by the New Albany–Floyd County Consolidated School System Board of Directors.

After the Scribners purchased the land from John Paul in 1813, they had control of all the ferries as far as their land extended. Ohio River ferries

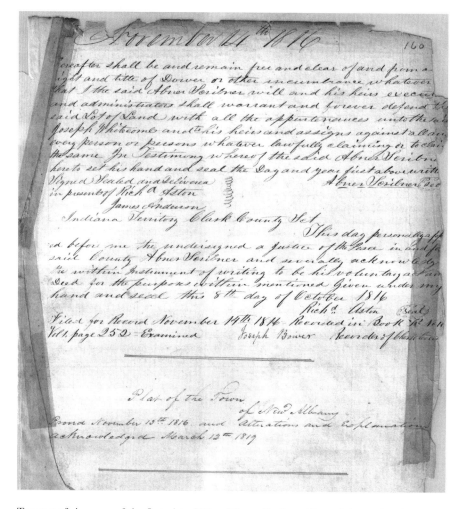

Two out of six pages of the first plat of New Albany. Scribner House is located at the southeast corner of Main and State Streets. *Courtesy Floyd County Surveyor, Plat Room, City-County Building, New Albany.*

were an important business as they provided the only public transit across the river. The Scribners established and ran a ferry themselves at the outset. It is believed that the first man to secure the right to run a ferry from the Scribners somewhat later was a Mr. Sproud. "Sproud the Ferryman" was a well-known character during the first years of the new town. Sproud's ferry landed at the foot of Upper Third Street. Horses working on a tramp wheel propelled the ferry.[3]

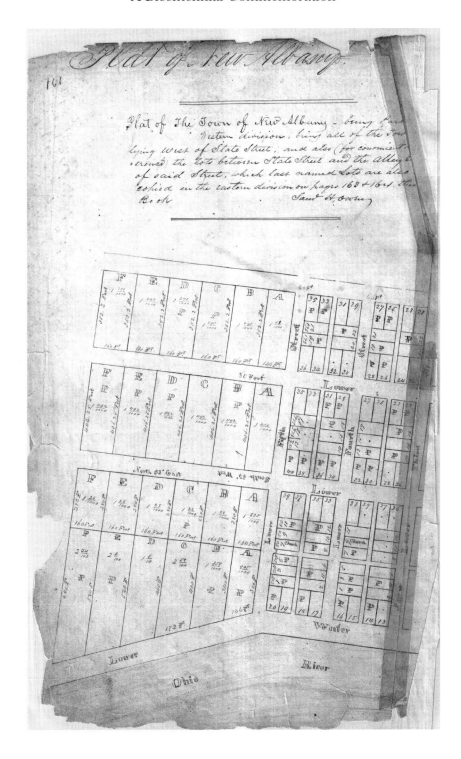

Even though the advertisement published by the Scribners in the eastern states did not allude to it, the truth of the matter was that the land was unhealthy for many years due to areas of stagnant water developing in town because streams that flowed down to the Ohio River from the surrounding hills could become backed up with fallen logs and brush.

Before any frame homes could be built, a sawmill and brickyard also had to be established. Joel and all the brothers were much occupied with advertising and developing New Albany. They advertised in numerous eastern cities through newspapers and broadsides. One of the advertisements, published in the *Columbian Centinel*, in Boston, Massachusetts, on September 11, 1813, read as follows:

 *New-Albany*

This Town, just laid out with spacious streets, public square, market, etc., is situated on the banks of the Ohio River, at the crossing place from Louisville to Vincennes, about two miles below the Falls, in the Indiana Territory, affords a beautiful and commodious harbor. The beauty of the prospect is not surpassed by any in the Western Country. The bank adjoining the river is high, and not subject to inundations. At the distance of 660 feet back is a second rise of about 20 feet, from which there is an extensive view up and down the river. There is a sufficient number of excellent and never-failing springs for the supplying of any number of inhabitants. This advantage, together with that of the country around, being dry, and clear of any stagnant water; being sufficiently distant below the Falls to avoid the fogs, and any noxious exhalement arising there from in the warm season: and the wind generally blowing up at that time, are sufficient reasons to induce a belief of the healthfulness of the situation. The advantages New Albany has in point of trade, are perhaps unrivalled by any on the Ohio, as it is immediately below all the dangers which boats and ships are subject to passing over the Falls, and is the only eligible situation for a depot all the exports and imports of a great part of the Territory, and may export and import while the river is low and markets good, as well as when the water is high. From the vast quantity of excellent ship timber, the abundance of iron ore, within a few miles, and the facility with which hemp is raised, it is presumed that this will be one of the best ports in the United States for the building of vessels, as well as for loading them. The erection of a sawmill to go by steam, is contemplated this fall, and a grist and flour mill next summer.

Lots will be sold at Auction on the first Tuesday and Wednesday in November next. The terms of payment will be one fourth ready money, and the remainder at three annual instalments, to be secured by deed of trust or otherwise. One fourth part of each payment to be paid into the hands of trustees, (to be chosen by the purchasers) until such payments shall amount to five thousand dollars; the interest of which to be applied to the use of schools in the town, for the use of its inhabitants forever.

Manufactures of iron, cotton, hemp, wool, etc. are much wanted, as are all kinds of mechanism.

The Proprietors,
New-Albany, July 8, 1813[4]

THE GENERATIONS OF SCRIBNER HOUSE OCCUPANTS

Joel Scribner, builder of the Scribner House, was New Albany's first postmaster. According to the recollections of Daniel Seabrook, who arrived in New Albany in 1814 and lived nearly a century until 1882, the first post office in New Albany, established in 1814, operated from a cabin at the southeast corner of Main and State Streets.[5] The mail came on Sunday morning when the carrier stopped on the way from Louisville to Vincennes. Joel was also appointed first clerk of the court in Floyd County. He served for more than four years until his death in 1823. His son, Harvey Scribner, followed him as clerk of the court. Harvey was also involved in the development of banking in New Albany and was the first secretary of the New Albany Insurance Company, chartered by the Indiana legislature in 1832. It later became the New Albany Banking Company.[6] Both Joel and his son, Harvey, are buried at Fairview Cemetery in New Albany.

Nathaniel followed Joel to Cincinnati in the fall of 1812. He was later involved with a group of people who developed proposals for a canal around the falls on the Indiana side of the Ohio River. The idea of a canal was promoted by Cincinnati businessmen to counter the profits being reaped by the portage of goods around the falls by businessmen on the Louisville side of the river. There was neither sufficient money nor labor for such an undertaking at the time, and it failed before it began. Nathaniel was active in promoting New Albany, organizing a trip in December 1818 to the new Indiana legislature at Corydon to petition for a new county to be created from parts of Clark and Harrison Counties and to make New Albany the county seat. Both petitions were successful, and thus Floyd County was formed. Tragically, Nathaniel fell ill on the way back from Corydon and died before he could reach home. He is buried at Fairview Cemetery. He left behind his widow, the former Elizabeth Edmonds, and their daughter Lucinda, age two. Later, Elizabeth married Dr. Asahel Clapp.

Abner also followed Joel, accompanying his brother Nathaniel to Cincinnati in the fall of 1812. All of the Scribner brothers were heavily invested in their attempt to start up the town of New Albany. Family letters reveal that in 1819 Abner was trying to find an investor to build a dry dock that would increase commerce in New Albany. He, in particular, had financial difficulties meeting debts incurred with the new town. He was away from New Albany and his family for long periods of time on various business ventures. It was Abner who made the trip downriver to New Orleans to collect the profits from a consignment of sugar sent by their brother Eliphalet from the West Indies. This was a loan to assist in the development of New Albany. The debt was in the amount of $8,000 for the shipment that arrived near New Orleans. Abner collected the money and returned upriver. Unfortunately for the buyer, General Dent, the ship sank in the river before it could be unloaded, a total loss to the purchaser.

Abner was particularly involved with the building of a large gristmill that failed due to defective equipment and not enough business in the region to support it at the time. He tried numerous things to recoup the debts owed. On April 25, 1825, he wrote a letter to his wife in New Albany, from on board the steamer *Caldonia*. He had purchased "Indian goods" to sell at Memphis, but his trunk had been broken into and money stolen.[7] He invested with a Mr. Davis in a cotton gin in Memphis, Tennessee. While attempting to reach a settlement with his partner, Abner fell ill and died on May 21, 1827, of yellow fever.[8] His widow, Charlotte Devol; their three children, namely, Bradford, Kate and Benjamin Scribner; and his stepson, Horatio Devol, survived him. Although Abner's wife and children never lived in the Scribner House, they were closely connected to it in various ways.

James Scribner, an older brother of Joel, Abner and Nathaniel, came to New Albany two or three years after the brothers first arrived. Records indicate his wife had died and that his two sons came with him. James arrived in time to be elected the first treasurer of the new Floyd County, and he held that post until his death in 1823. His son Alonson preceded him in death, and a second son, Isaac, went to St. Francisville, Louisiana, where he died at age twenty-two.[9]

SCRIBNER HOUSE NEIGHBORHOOD

Some of the earliest arrivals in New Albany reported that they boarded with the Scribners. Among them were Dr. Asahel Clapp and David Hedden. At some early time (we do not know exactly when), additional buildings went up on the lots between Scribner House and State Street, where the public garden belonging to Scribner House is now. At the back of the lot was a house built in the same style as Scribner House with rear galleries facing the river. The oldest DAR member, Wynema Wagoner, past regent, recalled in 2004 that when she was about twelve years old, the house was still in use as a boardinghouse for men. It was demolished about 1959. On the front corner lot, a brick building was constructed that a later generation referred to as the "Nathaniel Scribner House." By 1866, it housed "Scribner & Maginess, Dealers in Drugs."[10] The proprietor was Benjamin Scribner, son of Abner. Later, it had gasoline pumps installed in front. Eventually, the brick building was demolished and an auto service station occupied the front corner. All this indicates that Scribner House and its adjoining lots were the center of activity for many decades.

Sketch of the back of Scribner House by Walter H. Kiser. *Courtesy Indiana History Room, New Albany–Floyd County Public Library.*

DR. ASAHEL CLAPP, NEXT-DOOR NEIGHBOR

Dr. Asahel Clapp. *Courtesy Indiana History Room, New Albany–Floyd County Public Library.*

Dr. Asahel Clapp was next-door neighbor and brother-in-law of William Augustus Scribner. William studied medicine under Dr. Clapp, and in fact, for many years they practiced medicine together. Dr. Clapp was the first doctor in New Albany, arriving as a young man from Vermont. In 1819, he married Mary Lucinda Scribner, Joel's daughter, who died in childbirth the following year. Two years later, he married the widow of Nathaniel Scribner, the former Elizabeth Edmonds, and raised her daughter, Lucinda Ann, as his own. In the settlement of Nathaniel Scribner's estate, in order to satisfy debts, his widow was assigned Lot #3 on High Street.[11] This adjoins Lot #1, on which Scribner House stands. In 1822, Dr. Clapp constructed a brick house on the front eastern corner of Elizabeth's Lot #3. (This historic building has long been known as the South Side Inn Café.)

Dr. Clapp developed an extensive garden at the rear of the property; James Trueblood, an African American, worked for him as a gardener.[12] He also had other black servants in his household—namely, Amanda Finney, Josephine Mitchum and Charity Carter.[13] Dr. Clapp and Elizabeth had two children who survived infancy, Mary E. and William A. Clapp. William studied medicine and practiced in the same office in the house that his father had used.

Asahel Clapp had a distinguished career. The Indiana State Medical Society was formed in 1820 at Corydon, then the capital of the state, and Dr. Clapp was elected president. He was one of Indiana's most interesting citizens during his long residence in the state from 1817 until his death in

Scribner House, showing buildings on both sides. *Courtesy Piankeshaw Chapter DAR.*

1862. His diary, kept continuously from April 1819 until a few days before his death, is one of the most valuable contributions of its kind in the state. Every entry is prefaced by weather reports and thermometer and barometer readings. When the United States Weather Bureau was established at Louisville, Kentucky, in the 1870s, a copy of the diary was made for the bureau's use in order to make comparisons.[14]

Dr. Clapp's diary reveals his interest in the affairs of the community. For example, in 1820 he was the first fire chief of the first volunteer New Albany Fire Company. Above all, the diary reveals that his primary interests were in botany and geology. He was visited by Sir Charles Lyell, noted British geologist, who knew of Dr. Clapp's studies of the geology of the Falls of the Ohio. Many other famous visitors are also noted. His accounts of three extended journeys east in 1831, 1833 and 1835 show that scientists held him in high regard. He was entertained with great honor at Yale by the president and faculty. On these trips, he had occasion to visit in the home of Uriah Scribner, a relative of the New Albany Scribners.

Clapp's diary noted that in 1848 he mortgaged his house and was renting out rooms. Apparently, he was experiencing financial difficulties. In that year, he reported that the partnership with Dr. Scribner was dissolved, but he offered no other comment. It would have been about that time that his son, William A. Clapp, returned from medical school to practice in the office with his father. Dr. Asahel Clapp died in 1862 and is buried in Fairview Cemetery. Dr. William A. Scribner, who had been his partner, died in April 1868 and is also buried in Fairview Cemetery.

Many visitors to Scribner House have wondered when and how the three-story brick structure came to be built adjoining the corner of the old home. On July 11, 1868, the New Albany *Daily Commercial* reported on "…the fine building being constructed by Dr. William A. Clapp [son of Dr. Asahel Clapp] on the south side of Main Street. It will contain several fine business rooms and offices. The third story is to be finished as a Hall for Dudley Temple of Honor." Thus, we know that with Dr. Clapp's building and the Maginess & Scribner Drug Store, brick buildings fronting Main Street bordered both sides of the Scribner House yard by July 1868.

GRANDMOTHER PHEBE SCRIBNER'S HOUSE, LATER A PART OF HALE TAVERN

Dr. William Augustus Scribner's account of the family ceased with the 1828 death of his grandmother, Phebe Kellog Scribner, except for some notes added later about family church memberships. Research in the records of the Indiana Room of the New Albany–Floyd County Public Library verifies that his first wife, Caroline Chapman Scribner, died in 1837, at the time of the birth and death of a daughter, Anna Marie. He was left with three young children: Harvey, Caroline and Harriet Rowland Shields. Three years later in 1840, he married Harriet Partridge Hale of Pittsfield, Massachusetts, who apparently had come to visit her brother, Dr. David H. Hale, also originally from Pittsfield. Dr. Hale's wife was Esther Scribner, the aunt of William Augustus.

The Hales were proprietors of the famous Hale Tavern that was just down the street at the corner of West Third and High Streets. The large hotel had been constructed around the home originally built for Phebe Kellog Scribner, mother of the Scribner brothers. She had come to New Albany in 1814 to join her sons in the new settlement. After living a short time in a log cabin, Phebe built as her residence the central portion of what became

Hale Tavern from "A Pioneer Inn,"a pamphlet printed locally and written by Emma Carleton, August 1900. *Indiana History Room, New Albany–Floyd County Public Library.*

the Hale Tavern; it was the second frame dwelling erected in New Albany. In 1817, the first Presbyterian Church in New Albany was established in the back parlor of this house.

With David Hale as the proprietor of the Hale Tavern, the place became a social center for the town. The stage line between Louisville and St. Louis always made stops at the tavern door, and therefore many famous travelers stopped there, including Daniel Webster; Andrew Jackson; Martin Van Buren; William Henry Harrison; his grandson, former president Benjamin Harrison; Zachary Taylor; Oliver P. Morton; and many others.

In time, the Scribner House welcomed another set of children. These were the orphaned children of Dr. Scribner's daughter, Caroline, who had married James Shields on May 25, 1853. He was a grandson of Patrick Shields, the first settler in what is now Floyd County, who built a log house near the foot of the Knobs. The Shields family remained prominent in the affairs of the county through generations. Around 1928, Patrick's great-granddaughter Emma Nunemacher donated the stone doorstep of that log home to Scribner House, where it still serves its original purpose. James and Caroline Shields had four children: Esther "Ettie" Hale Shields, born in 1855; William Shields, born in 1858; Harriet Scribner Shields, born in 1861 and died in 1864 of scarlet fever; and Harvey Shields, born and died in 1864 at the time of their mother, Caroline's, death, only ten days after the death of her little daughter Hattie. The 1860 census shows the residents of the house to be Dr. William Augustus Scribner; his wife, Harriet; his son Harvey, a bank teller; his daughter Hattie, a music teacher; Charles Edward Scribner, age fourteen; Hattie Hale, age seventeen, born in Massachusetts; and Adaline von Moltwitz, age thirty-five, housekeeper.

After the death of their mother, Ettie, age about nine, and William, about six, came to live at Scribner House. Ettie and William were the orphaned children of Caroline Scribner. The 1870 census reveals that Dr. Scribner was gone and his wife, Harriet P. Scribner, was head of the household. In that same census, Harriet Rowland Scribner was listed without occupation; Charles Edward Scribner was twenty-four and secretary of the Ferry Company; Esther Shields was fourteen; William Shields was eleven; and Adaline von Moltwitz, age forty-three, was still the housekeeper. Charles Edward married Nannie Day in 1876. Sadly, he died of tuberculosis in 1879 at age thirty-three. His mother, Harriet Hale Scribner, died the year before in 1878. William Shields married a Ms. Keigwen, daughter of Colonel Keigwen, and moved to the Howard Park area. Their father, James Shields, was in business in New Albany, becoming involved with the glassmaking business of Captain John B. Ford, who manufactured the first plate glass in the United States. He followed Ford to the east where he was engaged for some years and then returned to New Albany. Like the Scribner family, he was a lifelong active member of the Presbyterian Church. During the last three years of his long life, he was confined in the hospital, and his funeral service in 1911 was conducted at the home of Ms. Hattie Scribner, where his daughter Ettie lived as an invalid. Mary Helen has told us much about Ettie and her teaching of young girls in the Busy Bees, which met weekly at Scribner House.

BENJAMIN FRANKLIN SCRIBNER

Although he never lived in the Scribner House, it is important to mention Benjamin Franklin Scribner, son of Abner Scribner. He was an influential citizen of New Albany and was closely connected to the Scribner House and those who lived there. Born in 1825, he was trained as a druggist and chemist but was always interested in military affairs. He was one of the original members of the Spencer Greys, which won honors on all occasions of competition with other companies of militia. In May 1846, the company was accepted in the Second Regiment of Volunteers. Benjamin was enrolled as a private. By the time the company had returned from its year of service in the War with Mexico, he was discharged as a sergeant. He had participated in the Battle of Buena Vista and had shown great valor. Upon his return to New Albany, he resumed his trade as a druggist. On December 20, 1849, he married Anna Martha Maginess, daughter of Dr. E.A. Maginess. They had ten children, seven of whom lived to adulthood.

At the outbreak of the Civil War, Benjamin became a colonel of the Seventh Regiment of the Indiana Militia and began drilling his men. On August 22, 1861, he raised a volunteer regiment at New Albany that became known as the Thirty-Eighth Indiana Volunteer Infantry. On September 21, 1861, the regiment joined General Rousseau, who was ordered to move on Muldraugh's Hill and Elizabeth, Kentucky, in order to intercept General Buckner, said to be moving on Louisville. The Thirty-Eighth Infantry was constantly occupied and engaged, and in the summer of 1862, Benjamin was put in command of a brigade that he led in the Battles of Perryville and Stone's River. At Perryville, his horse was shot out from under him, and he was wounded in the leg. He was engaged throughout the entire Tennessee Campaign and saw action in Georgia. After the Battle of Kennesaw Mountain, his health broke, and he was forced to resign his command on August 21, 1864, having been appointed brevet brigadier-general. After his resignation, he returned to New Albany and his drugstore business.

In January 1865, he was appointed collector of internal revenue for the Second District of Indiana and served in that office for eight years. In 1877, he was appointed U.S. commissioner in Alaska, but in 1878, he resigned this position and returned to New Albany, where he again became engaged in the drug business. As has been mentioned, his firm, Scribner & Maginess, was located on the corner of Main and State Streets, next to the Scribner House. Thus he was in daily contact with his cousin Miss Hattie Scribner and the other family members who lived there. He wrote several books describing his experiences in the Mexican War, the Civil War and Alaska. His primary work, *How Soldiers Were Made*, is an authoritative history of the Thirty-Eighth Regiment. Benjamin died in 1900 and is buried in Fairview Cemetery.

Scribner House Servants

An important member of the Scribner household was Adaline von Moltwitz. She came into the service of the Scribner family at about the age of eighteen. We do not know whether this was after Dr. Scribner married again or if she came earlier to help with his young children. She lived the rest of her long life there, taking care of house, children and garden. Adaline von Moltwitz died on December 24, 1907, at the Scribner house at the age of eighty-three after falling down a steep flight of stairs and breaking a hip.

Several of the Scribners had African American servants working for them. The 1820 census shows that Joel had a black female slave under the age of fourteen. The 1830 census shows that Harvey had a free black female between the ages of twenty and thirty years old living in his household. The 1840 census shows that Joel's daughter Julie Ann had two African American women living with her. In the same year, records show that William Augustus had one black male between the ages of ten and twenty-four years old living in his household. It should be noted that Dr. W.A. Clapp and William A. Scribner were instrumental in assisting African Americans in acquiring their freedom papers through the New Albany court system. W.A. Clapp testified in court on behalf of several African Americans, and W. A. Scribner was the clerk of court who signed many freedom papers.[15]

Miss Hattie Scribner and the Change of Ownership

By the turn of the twentieth century, Miss Hattie was still living in the house, as was her niece Esther (Ettie) H. Shields. At this time, Adaline von Moltwitz was still serving as caretaker of the house and family, but 1907 saw the death of Adaline. Ettie, who had been an invalid and confined to the house for many years, died on March 1, 1913. With the deaths of these two women, Miss Hattie was left alone.

The year 1913 was also the year of New Albany's Centennial celebration. Scribner House was open to the public for tours. Apparently, visitors were hard on the house and grounds, because the sum of $400 was given to Miss Hattie to help cover costs of repairing damage done during the tours. The *New Albany Daily Ledger* also featured an article regarding a ceremony at the graveside of the Scribners during the centennial celebration:

A Bicentennial Commemoration

Decorating Scribner Graves, Pioneer Descendants, Fireworks Program, Centennial Choir Tomorrow, Hattie Scribner's Sunday School, Centennial Service

An unpretentious little ceremony was carried out in the beautiful resting place of New Albany's dead, Fairview Cemetery. Friday afternoon the people in their enthusiasm over the centennial had apparently forgotten that in that place sleep the two Scribners, Nathaniel and Joel, while their brother, Abner, slumbers at Memphis. But Superintendent Lon Kelly had not forgotten and Friday afternoon, while the autumn sun was gilding the maple trees he, accompanied by Herman Rave, repaired to the quiet resting place and, in silence and reverence, planted two marker flags upon each of these two graves, so that they may easily be found by those who should wish to honor their deaths. Next to Joel lies his wife, who survived him 10 years and then his children, Harvey, Lucy, Eliphalet and Harriett, all of whom died young. Dr. Scribner lists all his siblings in his journal and speaks of the death of his brother Eliphalet. Then comes the grave of Nathaniel and to the left of him sleep Dr. Asahel Clapp and his wife.

It is probably not generally known that these people were first buried in a cemetery on State near Spring Street but were removed to their present location in 1840.[16]

Several other articles appeared in the centennial special edition of the *Ledger*, including "Miss Hattie Scribner's Home is 99 Years Old," "New Albany's One Hundredth Birthday Welcomed With Booming Cannon" and "Continuous Program of Joyous Festivities Will Mark Celebration." One program included a reenactment of the landing of the three Scribner brothers at the foot of Pearl Street. It was done by Edward, Richard and Frank Scribner of Indianapolis, great-grandsons of Abner.

One day during the festivities was designated "Hattie Scribner Day." A *Ledger* article about the day reads as follows:

One of the interesting centennial features of yesterday was the reception for Miss Hattie Scribner at First Presbyterian church at the morning service. Miss Scribner, granddaughter of Joel Scribner, one of the three Scribner brothers, founders of the town, was the first teacher of the primary class in the First Church Sunday School. She was instructor for nearly half a century, retiring a few years ago, and over 1,100 children passed under her care.

Scribner family plot located in Fairview Cemetery, New Albany. *Photo by K. Holwerk.*

Plaque dedicated to the Scribner family located at grave site. *Photo by Curt Peters.*

𝔉irst 𝔓resbyterian 𝔆hurch

New Albany, Indiana

THE HATTIE SCRIBNER DAY

Welcome

Hattie Scribner featured on First Presbyterian Church bulletin during New Albany's centennial celebration. *Courtesy Indiana History Room, New Albany–Floyd County Public Library.*

Short talks were made by Mrs. D.F. Boxman, Charles D. Knoefel and George Stephens, former pupils, and the Rev. E.C. Lucas read a letter from Samuel A. Culbertson of Louisville, also a former pupil, regretting his inability to be present. Mrs. W.A. Hedden sang "Light in the Window" and a class of children sang "Dare to Do Right" an old time song that had been taught by Miss Scribner.

Interesting reminiscences of the school and of the Scribner family were given by Miss Scribner. She gave the names of a number of couples who had attended the primary school when they were little children and later married. An audience that filled the church to its capacity attended the service, and when Miss Scribner asked her former pupils to stand nearly one-half the assemblage rose to their feet.[17]

Scribner descendants at New Albany's centennial in 1913. *Courtesy Piankeshaw Chapter DAR.*

Miss Hattie sold Scribner House to Piankeshaw Chapter Daughters of the American Revolution in May 1917, with arrangement for her to live there for the remainder of her life. On September 8, 1917, the daughters met in their new home, with Miss Hattie reading her paper, "The Battle of Buena Vista," to the DAR chapter. Miss Hattie's cousin Colonel Benjamin F. Scribner had taken an active part in that battle.

On September 20, 1917, before another meeting, Miss Hattie was called to her heavenly reward. So ended the 103-year residence of the Scribner family in the old house and so began a new chapter in the life of New Albany's homeplace with the dedicated care of the house by the Daughters of the American Revolution.

Chapter 3
"The Old House Speaks"

by Mary Helen Scribner

Mary Helen Scribner, great-granddaughter of Joel Scribner, was the daughter of Harvey Scribner, son of Dr. William Augustus Scribner. Born in 1879, she died February 21, 1972, at age ninety-three. For more than thirty-five years, she taught first grade at Silver Street Elementary School in New Albany. She lived in New Albany until her marriage in 1964 to John Rothwell. After his death, she returned from St. Petersburg, Florida, to live in New Albany. She was a member of St. John's United Presbyterian Church, the Daughters of the American Revolution and the Tourist Club of New Albany.

Mary Helen wrote two papers about the Scribner House. She wrote the first, "The Old House Speaks," under the name Mary Helen Scribner. It was published in booklet form with illustrations and sold in the Scribner House gift shop.[18] Later she wrote "Personalities of Scribner House As I Knew Them," under her married name, Mary Helen Scribner Rothwell. The paper was read at the October 14, 1950, meeting of Piankeshaw Chapter. Thus we have beautiful and personal firsthand accounts about the house and those who lived in it during her lifetime.

In "The Old House Speaks," Mary Helen recorded her memories of Scribner House as though the house itself was speaking. It is easy for the reader, therefore, to get caught up in the activities surrounding Scribner House as seen through its very own "eyes and ears."

Madam Regent and Members of the Piankeshaw Chapter, Daughters of the American Revolution:

I have been asked by some of your members to tell my story. I have never kept a diary but I will try to recall as much of my life as I can.

Scribner House sketch by James Russell. *Courtesy Piankeshaw Chapter DAR.*

I first came to consciousness of the fact that I was to be in the Spring of 1814. My Master, Joel Scribner and Mary Bull, his wife, had come to New Albany on the second day of May 1813, and with the William Waring family had been living in a double log cabin near Sixth and High Street.

Neither family being small, the cabin was crowded, and there was much talk about a new home being needed. Then when trees were cut to make room for me, I knew that I would soon make my start in life.

Sugar maples, poplars, and beautiful shiny birch trees, all had to come down, and a thick undergrowth of green brier, spicewood, and pawpaw had to be cleared away. It would hurt me now to hear the ring of the ax in those grand old trees, but then, like all youngsters, I was only impatient to get started and was filled with excitement when I knew that my cellar was being dug and my basement and three stories were going up.

At first I was too young to realize that I was any different from the other houses that were scattered down High Street, but as I grew I began to notice a certain distinction in my make up. They were using bricks in my wall instead of logs, and covering them with sawed boards. I heard little William say that I was to be the first frame house in town, and at that I began to hold my head a wee bit higher.

Well, the family moved in. There were my master, Joel Scribner, my mistress Mary Bull Scribner and their children, Harvey, William Augustus, Lucy Maria, Mary Lucinda, Eliphalet, Julia Ann, and Phebe. I thought that quite enough of a family for me to shelter, but in a little over a year, I saw some very fine sewing being done, by hand in those days, embroidery, wee tucks, puffs, cording and all. Then one night I was awakened by a tiny wail, and I knew that I had another to care for. Little Harriet Naomi had arrived.

Yes, I know that they all thought they owned me, and cared for me. I've heard them do a lot of talking about keeping house, but it has always been the other way around—I've kept them, every one and cared for them, from my first master to my last mistress. I've held their babies, helped them fight the croup, watched over them as they grew up, listened in on their love affairs, planned their weddings, and taken the whole responsibility of the family on my shoulders.

I even started them to school and to church. If it had not been for me, Miss Lucy could not have taught school in my front room down stairs where little girls looked out of the window at the wood choppers instead of doing their sums.

And when for some reason the Presbyterian Church could not hold its meeting as was its custom in the High Street House, I offered them my best room and the family just couldn't get out of going to meeting when it was held in the very house in which they lived.

But to go back to the school, there was a little girl named Harriet who came to Miss Lucy. She was a good little girl, too, but one day she went through my dining room just at noon. There were some hot boiled potatoes on the sideboard. I saw her take one and eat it. I knew that her mother would be grieved, for in those days children were taught that to take the smallest thing without asking was stealing. And sure enough her mother sent her back the next day to tell aunt Polly, that's what they called my mistress, all about it, and to say that she was sorry, and I heard my mistress say: "Why child, whenever you are hungry just tell aunt Polly and you shall have something to eat."

Then it was just tell Aunt Polly, later it was just tell Adaline, for we always loved children and from the time the cooking was done by the great open fire place in my basement dining room down to the days of the wood stove in the outside kitchen there must always be something for them to eat.

When the children of the fourth generation visited me on the Sabbath Day between Sunday School and Church there would always be a plate of something for them on the stand in the front room upstairs. Sometimes it was good homemade bread, butter and sugar cut in thin strips and piled log cabin fashion. Sometimes it was crisp sugary cookies, and sometimes the most delicate angelfood layer cake with quince jelly filling. That last was Adaline's make and the most delicious I ever tasted.

Oh I can brag, for after Ad came I never did the cooking myself, but just kept an eye on her to see if I could discover any of her secrets.

And secrets she must have had for there were never fried potatoes like hers. Fried potatoes in the blue dish, light rolls, light biscuits she called them, pickled pears, Spanish cream and coffee—that was a supper fit for a king, and anyone who ate of that supper once ever after talked of Ad's fried potatoes in the blue dish.

And cookies, the best that anyone ever ate. I nearly burst with indignation to this day when I think of how she used to bake cookies over in the summer kitchen and how almost before she got the pan out of the oven there would be two or three of the youngsters waiting to eat one of those precious cookies. Once, it seems to me, they took two or three apiece out of each pan. How she ever had enough left out of a batch to fill a cookie jar, I don't see.

But as usual I am getting ahead of my story. Long before this a number of my master's family had followed him West. His brothers, Abner and Nathaniel, had come while he was in Cincinnati, before my day, but I was old enough to remember quite plainly how glad we all were to see his mother, Phebe, his brother, James, and his sister Elizabeth. I felt relieved of a great responsibility when his mother came, for I knew, mother-like, she would help more than any one else with the morals of the family and especially with the bringing up of the grandchildren. I was glad that she was there when young William decided to go to Cincinnati with his uncle.

Nathaniel was going to New York on business, and as there were no steamboats running on the river here, and no public conveyances of any sort, the trip as far as Cincinnati had to be made on horseback. When William took it into his head to go that far with his uncle to bring back the horses, it seemed to me too long and lonely a trip for a lad of fifteen but his grandmother seemed to think him quite a man and quite responsible enough to travel alone. She was right for he made the trip, three days there and three days back, in safety.

And I always was glad that Mr. Nathaniel made that trip to New York for when he returned in the fall he brought his sister Esther with him and Miss Elizabeth Edmonds. It did not take me long to decide that that business trip had been a successful one. He and Miss Elizabeth were married very soon. In 1818 Mr. Nathaniel went to Corydon with Mr. John Graham, the surveyor, to see what could be done about a new county, for at that time we were still in Clark County. The petition for the county was granted but Mr. Nathaniel was taken desperately ill and when the family reached him he was beyond all hope of recovery.

In 1822 young William left us again, this time to practice medicine in Paoli. Having studied with Dr. Asahel Clapp and been examined by the medical board at Charlestown, he started off with all the assurance of a young M.D. Though I must confess that when he wrote to us of visiting one patient with intermittent fever, one with remittent and one sick child, three patients in town and one in the country I felt almost as uneasy about him as I did when he started for Cincinnati, but I need not have given myself so much concern. He proved fully able to care for himself and others.

At Paoli he made friends with a certain Thomas Chapman who, half in fun and half in earnest, promised him his youngest sister for a wife. Thomas died while taking a boatload of produce from Leavenworth to New Orleans but his two sisters, receiving the melancholy intelligence of his death, deemed it their duty to him to visit his family. That was the winter of 1826, so bitter cold that it chills me now to think of it. The young ladies traveled as far as Cincinnati quite comfortably. But by that time the cold was so intense that the Ohio River was frozen over and as a public conveyance coming this way was a rarity they had to remain there for several weeks.

One day a spring wagon drawn by four horses stopped at a public house across from the Chapman home. It was to carry congressmen as far as Cincinnati and return empty unless passengers for the return trip were found. The driver being very much of a gentleman, Mrs. Chapman felt that the problem of her would-be guests was solved and sent a letter written by Dr. William, requesting the sisters to return with him. This they did and I judge that Caroline Matilda must have approved her brother's promise, as did the doctor, for it was only the next October that I saw Ned and Trim, the doctor's horses come dashing in State Street, turn the corner and stop at my front gate. It was just at sunset. The sky was still blue, blue with red and gold clouds banked over the knobs in the west. It was one of those brilliant pictures October always brings me but I remember that as the doctor helped Miss Matilda from the buggy I thought that no sky could rival the brightness of their faces. I suspected that we would have a wedding and I was not mistaken.

You can see it on the records, William Augustus Scribner and Caroline Matilda Chapman were married at New Albany, Indiana, October 25, A.D. 1827.

Oh there were plenty of weddings in the family. It was hard to escape them with so many good looking young folks about. Of course Miss Lucy never married for she kept school, but Mary Lucinda married Dr. Asahel Clapp, the Botanist. Julia Ann married Rev. Leander Cobb and in due season became the Grandmother of Anne Cobb, the dialect poet of the Kentucky mountains. Phebe married James Cooper Davis. She was the mother of your own Chapter member, Mrs. Mary Scribner Collins.

I felt just like the mother about all those weddings. I could hardly wait to see the children happily married, but when they left me I was too lonely for words. I was glad therefore, when after five years more of practice in Paoli the young doctor went into partnership with Dr. Clapp, and with his wife came back to me. They brought little Harvey with them from Paoli, but before long he grew too big to be the baby, so we had to get another, Caroline Sophia, and when she had outgrown the baby clothes they were handed down to Harriet Rowland.

When dear little Anna Maria came, she and my mistress both left us and we were very lonely for awhile, but before very long Harriet Partridge Hale consented to come and be a second mother as the children called her. They never allowed any one to call her a stepmother for she always said that she was a real mother to them, and as far as I could see she was.

Her own Charles Edward was a big boy before he knew that Harvey, Caroline and Harriet were not his own brother and sisters. Eddie always was a lively chap and from the time he could talk, liked to make folks laugh. He was quite a musician. Mr. Nutting, whose silver band had taken prizes at both New Orleans and Boston, taught him to play the snare drum and he

Harriet Partridge Hale Scribner, second wife of Dr. W.A. Scribner, by George Morrison. *Photo by Mel Underhill. Courtesy Piankeshaw Chapter DAR.*

in turn taught nearly every snare drummer in town.

He was a great mimic too and if a comic stunt was wanted at an entertainment, I knew before hand that he would do it, or part of it with Mr. Haskins to help. Many is the concert we've gotten ready for at our house. Miss Hattie used to have a singing school of her own. All the children in town belonged, it seemed to me, at least all I ever heard of. Then she played for the choral society when Mr. Siegfried was leader. I can just see her yet the way she looked when she went to a concert.

She had the prettiest dresses. The one I liked best was white silk pineapple tissue with crossbars of pink. It was made a full skirt with three wide flounces, a gathered waist with round low neck and short puffed sleeves. There was narrow pink silk fringe on the flounces and at the edge of the neck and sleeves. Miss Hattie had a pretty plump neck and with her beautiful chestnut brown hair brushed smooth, braided and done in a coil, fastened with two gold hair balls, she looked to me like one of the pinks out of our own garden.

Talking of how Miss Hattie looked reminds me that I thought I was rather fine looking myself in those days. I was always painted white and my shutters were of a dark shady green. We used to close the shutters on hot days and turn the slats to let the breeze from the river blow through. To step into the hall from the street on a summer day was like stepping into a cool shady glen. My front windows were short like my back ones. I rather liked them short myself. I thought they were more in keeping with my style of beauty.

I've heard folks say that my floors are hard wood. I'm not sure about that but if they are, would they not refinish beautifully?

Nursery windowsill. *Photo by K. Holwerk.*

At first my third story was not finished, and when Harvey used to sleep there he would wake up on winter mornings to find snow on his coverlid. Did you ever notice the window on the east side of that room? It looks like a dormer window but it is really built through the big chimney. That chimney is really a curiosity for it takes care of all the flues from the basement to the attic. It begins as though it were going to be two chimneys on the east side of the cellar and basement dining room. Each is built up through the first and second stories and attic and then they unite in an arch over the attic window into the one big chimney you see on my roof. That attic window was the favorite playhouse for all the children of the later generations.

Phebe's granddaughter and Harvey's daughter used to play there by the hour with a big box full of little china dolls, doll dishes and sewing materials. They were the greatest girls to want to stay all night. It never rained too hard for them to come to me but if one drop fell at going home time, it was excuse enough for them to stay and they would sleep with Miss Esther in the big cherry bed.

My back porch upstairs was the next favorite spot. There were awnings to keep the sun off and that made it the finest place to play and read. When the awnings were down there was the river to watch with its ferry boats going over to Portland and the big packets coming up from Evansville. From there we used to watch the fireworks from the Louisville Exposition on Fourth Street. Oh things were never dull on my back porch. The one downstairs was for company. That's where folks came to see the night blooming cereus and where they gathered after missionary meetings and Busy Bee annual meetings.

My parlor was pretty too. I can think of nothing more cheerful than my parlor in winter with the bright fire and the bracket lamps on each side of the chimney: The rosy carpet and my lovely old mahogany furniture. The paper in the parlor used to be just the right background for mahogany furniture too. It was blue-gray with stripes about three inches wide made up of little gold lines and between the stripes were white medallion-like figures edged with gold.

At the windows there were white embroidered muslin curtains looped back over round silver curtain holders and in summer it was just as cool and delightful with the breeze from the river as any spot could be.

My front yard was a pretty place too. The brick walls on either side never spoiled it for they were always covered with vines and close to them were annual roses and a big pink moss rose bush.

In early days there was an arbor over the front walk where the old fashioned honeysuckle grew and bloomed in delicate creamy fragrant clusters. There was a border bed on either side of the walk from this arbor to the front door. Next to the arbor were tall white lilies and at the end of the bed by the house were two large red peonies.

The back yard was a delight to me for it was so beautiful and at the same time so full of places for my children to play. The rockery with its ferns, the pond with its gold fish, pond lilies and large umbrella plant in the center. The grape arbor with its close clusters of sweetest Delawares, and underneath it the bed of lilies of the valley. In the center of the yard was a round bed of tuberoses and rose geraniums, and at each end of that, the tight little red and gold dahlias. But best of all was the border bed beside the board walk. There is a sense of something so lovely that I just want to shut my eyes and breathe when I think of the crepe myrtle that grew there, and the memory of the tea rose too, makes me catch my breath. But the other flowers, the purple columbine, the bleeding heart, the sweet William, touch-me-nots, rose moss, and Johny-jumpups make me think of children skipping happily and calling to one another. How they loved the bunch of everlasting plant. They would take a leaf and press it together until they separated the two sides and then blow it up like a glove finger.

But there, I am quite out of breath, and out of order too, I am afraid, talking so much about myself. But I am so excited and so happy that I could sing for joy. A few years ago I thought I was never to be anything but a shabby old building. But now I just wish I had a great big looking glass so I could turn and turn and look at my new coat of paint, green shutters and all, and my beautiful porches. I want to look again and again at my fireplaces and the dear little table that came across the mountains with my family. Many is the time I've been afraid some one would chop it up for kindling wood. But it is safe with all the other lovely things you have given back to me and all I can do to thank you is to say that I will try to take as good care of the D.A.R. as I did of my own family.

Chapter 4

"Personalities of Scribner House As I Knew Them"

by Mary Helen Scribner Rothwell

"Personalities" was written by Mary Helen Scribner Rothwell, great-granddaughter of Joel Scribner.[19] *In helping to keep the history of the Scribner family and the house fresh and alive, "Personalities" was read by Miss Carrie Beers at the Fifty-Second Anniversary of the establishment of the Piankeshaw Chapter DAR, October 14, 1950. Mary Helen Scribner Rothwell's recollections in her very own words follow.*

I hardly know where to begin this story of my personal recollections of the people who lived in the Scribner House, but I might ask this question and find the answer, a starting point.

What was it that made going down to Aunt Hattie's the most to be desired event in the life of a child of seven or eight? Was it the house itself? Of course that had its attractions. The fragrance of baking cookies, when one stepped in at the front door, the coolness in summer from the river breeze, the warmth in winter from stoves glowing on each floor, the back porches where one could play, or watch the boats on the river or the Dinky train coming from Louisville every thirty minutes, the flower lined board walk leading to the back gate, and the third floor with its box of little china dolls, all were a part of an influence that lasts a life time. But what of the personalities that breathed the breath of life into these inanimate things.

"The Girls" my father called them. To me, they were Aunt Hattie, Cousin Ettie and Add. Aunt Hattie was Miss Harriet Rowland Scribner, daughter of Dr. William Augustus Scribner, whose portrait hangs over the mantel, and granddaughter of the builder of the Scribner House, Joel. I suppose when I first remember her she was about fifty years old, half a head shorter than I am now. She used to enjoy telling of the little mission schoolboy who looked up at her and said, "Missus, didn't you never grow no bigger[?]" She dressed very plainly, always in black, brown, or grey, a close fitting hat or bonnet and warm Kashmir shawls for winter, with earmuffs for very cold weather. But her clothing had not always been so subdued. In fact, it had been quite gay when she had been accompanist for the Choral Club, and when her own singing classes gave their concerts—as scarves, fans, and a number of gay dresses in the old trunk would testify, for she had been quite a popular musician. My mother has often told me of doing Aunt Hattie's hair for these musicals. She had a quantity of beautiful brown hair that my mother, even before she was her sister-in-law, loved to braid and wind around her head. I think there is a black and magenta headdress that she wore on such occasions in the glass case up stairs.

But to come back to my recollection of Aunt Hattie. She still had a large class of piano pupils, taught the infant class in the First Presbyterian Church, and was a worker in the Missionary Society from the time the joint society was formed in the three Presbyterian churches. From the testimony of many of her pupils, I think her greatest influence in the community was through the teaching of the infant class, as a class of all children under nine years of age was called in those days. Every year she gave a Bible to every pupil who for that year had recited two Bible verses each Sunday, and I have heard many older people say with pride that they still kept Miss Hattie's Bible. Mr. Sam Culbertson bragged to her one day, "Miss Hattie, I still have the Bible you gave me." "Yes, and it is as good as new," said his wife. "Now, Louise, it's pretty well thumbed," he answered.

I cannot begin to tell of all of the things that add up to show Aunt Hattie's staunch, sturdy, Christian character, or that quality of firmness that made her seem very positive. This very positiveness was for the right, and therefore, a great virtue, for a child did not think of demurring when she said "That will do" or "That is not quite genteel," but felt it was highly necessary to do and be what would keep one in her good graces to later deserve her respect and esteem. She herself, was held in great esteem and respect by all who knew her.

Cousin Ettie, the second in the naming of this trio, though not by any means the second in my affections, was Miss Esther Hale Shields, daughter of James Shields and Caroline Scribner Shields. Carrie Scribner, was also

Clothing items that belonged to Miss Hattie Scribner. *Photo by K. Holwerk.*

Dr. William Scribner's daughter, coming in age between my father and Aunt Hattie. James Shields was a cousin of my mother's (Mary Day) and therefore Cousin Ettie was my double cousin and doubly dear to me. I do not know how old she was when her mother died and she and her younger brother, William, came to live at the Scribner House with Grandfather and his second wife Harriet Hale, whose portrait is over the parlor mantel. Let me say in passing, that my father, Harvey, Aunt Carrie and Aunt Hattie were children of Dr. Scribner and his first wife, Caroline Matilda Chapman, a descendant of Dr. Fuller of the Mayflower. Uncle Ed, the boy in the portrait of the boy and the dog, was the son of Dr. Scribner and his second wife. About thirty-two, when I first remember her, Cousin Ettie was like a second mother to me, for it was she who cared for me the days I spent there, and it was she with whom I slept on the many happy nights I spent at the Old House.

There are a few left in New Albany who would remember Miss Ettie for the Busy Bee Home Mission Band she organized. But there are many who would trace their interest in missions to that band. My older sister, Tillie, May Collins (Hawk), Nellie Day, Frankie McCurdy (Tyler), Bessie Beers (Everest), Mary and Sarah Rogers, were among the older girls and later, Edith Collins, Jennie and Alice Devol, Myrtle Anthony, Abbie Main Waring, Bertha Schueler (Van Pelt) and others whom I do not remember, formed the Little Busy Bees.

Charles Edward "Little Eddie" Scribner, by George Morrison. *Courtesy Piankeshaw Chapter DAR.*

I wish in some way, I could convey to you the delight we took in those meetings. Each band held their meeting every other Saturday afternoon. That meant that every Saturday afternoon, Cousin Ettie devoted her time to interesting young girls and children in missions.

I suppose many of you do not remember the Nathaniel Scribner house that stood on the corner where the filling station is now. The two back rooms of that house, with the basement under them, were used by the William Scribner family and opened onto the brick hill. One of those rooms was kept as the Busy Bee Room. In it, was a chest of drawers with materials for our fancy work, and a bookshelf for our mission books. I think our interest was held by the fancy work of all kinds Cousin Ettie taught us to do, while she read to us some book on the needs of children of different countries and the mission work done there. Our annual meeting was a great event. Our fancy work was displayed on a table in the music room, to be bought by our parents and friends, and in the parlor the girls, in white dresses, blue ribbon badges fastened on with tuberoses and a rose geranium leaf, sat in two straight rows facing our audience, also seated in straight rows, and gave a missionary program. We gave $32.00 a year for the education of a little girl in Alaska. The last years of her life, Cousin Ettie suffered from some kind of paralysis, beginning with difficulty in walking and ending in years in a wheel chair and finally in bed, but always bright and cheerful, never complaining, she was an inspiration to all who visited her.

A Bicentennial Commemoration

Who was responsible for the smell of cookies as we opened the front door? That was Adaline von Moltwitz. I remember being heartily laughed at when at about four, I asked if I shouldn't call her Miss. I could hardly understand why it should be Aunt Hattie, Cousin Ettie and just plain Ad, when she was the oldest of the three, but she was well satisfied with just the plain name, though I know she thought the "von" in her name denoted descent from nobility. She certainly belonged to nobility, for a truer more devoted or loyal friend a family never had. She came to do the housework for the family when she was about 15 years old and stayed as the very heart of the home until she died of a broken hip in her eighties.

Many of the attractions of the home trace back to Ad. It was Ad who made the flower border by the boardwalk and kept the little greenhouse. It was Ad who baked the good bread and rolls, made the Spanish cream, pickled pears, fried potatoes for the blue dish, made the mince pies and fruit cake for Thanksgiving and Christmas, and always beat you calling out "Christmas gift" when you opened the front door on Christmas morning. She may not have planned the surprises for the children's teas, but she carried them out. She was very fond of children.

Edith Collins and I used to look forward to spending a week of our vacation at Aunt Hattie's and always one evening, several of our little friends were invited to take tea with us. On those occasions, there was often a little surprise of some kind. One time the first plate of biscuits had a tiny, china doll baked in them.

The two events of the year were Christmas and a night in mid-summer when the night-blooming cereus would open. That was a gala night spent on the lower porch with friends and neighbors awaiting and watching the opening of the lovely flower.

At Christmas, just the Scribners would be invited for the usual turkey dinner, but in the afternoon, Cousin Mary Collins' family would arrive for tea, bringing their Christmas gifts to be added to those already waiting on the mahogany tables in the parlor. For tea, there would be turkey salad, hot rolls, spiced peaches, Spanish cream and fruitcake. After tea, the parlor doors would be opened, Aunt Hattie would play Boxes March on the piano, while the children and any oldsters who had marching feet, would join in a march around the rooms. Then we would sit in an expectant circle around the grate fire and wait our turn to open our gifts.

I have tried to picture to you the occupants of the Scribner House as I remember them. If you would go farther back, read again "The Old House

Concert program from Miss Hattie's class held at
Woodward Hall, 1864. *Courtesy Piankeshaw Chapter DAR.*

Speaks" for this house was always the home of Joel Scribner and his children
and his children's children, to the third and fourth generation and when the
Daughters of the American Revolution moved into the House, they were
taken into its family—"A Goodly Heritage," "A Goodly Fellowship."

Chapter 5

History of Piankeshaw Chapter Daughters of the American Revolution

It is important to include here a history of the establishment of Piankeshaw Chapter DAR because the daughters not only purchased Scribner House in 1917 as a meeting place but have also lovingly preserved and cared for it ever since as a museum dedicated to the founders of New Albany. They have made it available to the community to learn about its history and enjoy its hospitality. It is a unique historic treasure, for few communities have so preserved the first frame house in the town, built by one of the founders of the town, and now the oldest structure in the town. It was lived in by the Scribner family through four generations during 103 years and preserves many of the original furnishings of the family. Such historic preservation is one of the goals of the National Society of the Daughters of the American Revolution.

GETTING ORGANIZED

The organizational meeting of Piankeshaw Chapter Daughters of the American Revolution was held on October 15, 1898. The original minutes of that meeting have been preserved by the chapter and, in part, read as follows:

> *It was a typical mid-autumn day when the "Daughters of the American Revolution" started on their long contemplated excursion to the rural home*

DAR insignia.

of Miss Annabelle Smith. October flung out her royal banners, unlocked her generous store, and spread her treasures on the way. A clear sky, warm, mellow sunshine, fragrant clumps of forest, a perfect road, and a wagon full of enthusiastic women, beckoned at the outset the happy gala spirit which was to brood over the occasion. Even the most sedate "daughters" upon whose heads there lay the touch of two score years and more, took on a festive air, as the city's hum was left behind; and how shall I record the riot of fun and mirth into which the younger "daughters" plunged. Without incident or adventure the journey continued.

Miss Smith had timely warning of the near approach of these daughters of martial history—for on the autumn air had been carried their significant war cry, and strange to record, the well-known voice of her Regent above the din, fell reassuringly on her ear. Miss Smith was equal to the onslaught and very composedly met the invaders, surrendering herself and home to their mercy.

Promptly the meeting opened with the usual prayer in concert, and the singing of our national hymn, "America," Miss Smith presiding at the piano. Official reports of Secretary and Treasurer followed. After a few introductory remarks by the Regent, Mrs. Maginness read the constitution and by-laws. After considering the import of each article, the members adopted the whole as formulated.

The Regent read the names of those whose official papers had been returned—making in all eighteen charter members, with some others very near the entrance door.

Charter members were: Miss Mary E. Cardwill, Mrs. Ann E. Evens, Mrs. Frances Rice Maginness, Miss Estelle Kinder Sowle, Miss Francis M. Hedden, Mrs. Martha T. H. Gwin, Miss Anna E. Cardwill, Miss Emma C. Dewhurst, Mrs. Helen Fawcett, Miss Theodosia Hedden, Mrs. Anna E. H. Greene, Mrs. Margaret Johnson (Sieboldt), Miss Carrie B. Webster, Miss Annabelle Smith (Hartley), Miss Susan Eleanor Hooper, Miss Alice L. Greene, Miss Anna Fitch Bragdon, Miss Clara Kimball Bragdon and Miss Clara Funk.

Officers elected were: Regent: Miss Mary Cardwill; Vice-Regent: Mrs. Frances Rice Maginness; Secretary: Mrs. Helen Mar Fawcett; Treasurer: Miss Anna E. Cardwill; Registrar: Miss Fannie M. Hedden; Historian: Mrs. Martha T. H. Gwin.

As the hours of this perfect day would not tarry, the "Daughters" with lingering adieus to their kind hostess turned their faces city-ward, and in the beautiful autumn gloaming, wearing the dignity of fresh found honors, the new-born chapter went merrily back to home and duty. Melody floated out on the evening air as one patriotic song after another was heartily sung—for had not been born that afternoon, October 15, 1898, about the hour of 3:00 p.m., at the country home of Miss Annabelle Smith on Grant Line Road, the "New Albany Chapter of the Daughters of the American Revolution."[20]

The actual beginning of the local DAR chapter started with the election of Judge George B. Cardwill, brother of Mary Cardwill, to the Indiana legislature in 1894–95. He was a member of the Sons of the American Revolution and attended a meeting of that organization in Indianapolis, Indiana, during the year. There he met Mrs. C. Foster, state regent of the DAR. When his sister came to visit, a meeting was arranged, and Mrs. Foster urged Miss Cardwill to organize a chapter in New Albany. For three years, it was little more than a dream, but Miss Cardwill, in her enthusiastic manner, never let the idea die.

Perhaps one of the most notable meetings of the chapter was the charter meeting held at the home of the Heddens in Dewey Heights in December 1898. Their parlor was decorated in American flags, and members were brought to the Hedden home in an old-fashioned stagecoach. Many of the women dressed in costumes impersonating various historical women of the revolutionary period. For example, Mrs. Frank Greene came dressed as Martha Washington in a gown of green brocade with a pretty lace cap over powdered hair. Mrs. Frances Maginness wore a black dress of silk and lace representing Mrs. Israel Putnam, and Mrs. Thomas Jefferson was there in the person of Fannie Hedden. Miss Theo Hedden came as Mrs. Benjamin Franklin, Annebelle Smith was dressed as Betsy Ross and Mrs. Abigail Adams was represented by Carrie B. Webster.

The regent presented the charter to the chapter with these words:

Members of the New Albany Chapter, it is now my pleasant duty, as your regent, to present to you, by the authority of the National Society of the Daughters of the American Revolution, this charter, the sign and seal of our association, as a chapter, with the national body. Cherish it now and hereafter, not only as a token of an outward connection with a great patriotic institution, but also as an emblem of an inner spiritual union, in behalf of American patriotism, which it is our province and your privilege to foster.[21]

A Bicentennial Commemoration

The chapter had temporarily chosen the name New Albany Chapter of the DAR, and it was at this meeting that a committee presented the name Piankeshaw as the appropriate one for adoption. The committee members chose the name for several reasons. Before Indiana became a state, it was the Piankeshaws, a part of the great Algonquin Tribe, who used this part of Indiana as their hunting ground. They were referred to as the "Open Door" of the Wabash because they controlled the traffic of that river. The hope of the founders was that the chapter would ever be an "Open Door" to historical research, always bring attention to people and places of local historical importance and to thoughts and deeds of patriotism. Secondly, the Piankeshaws gave material aid to George Rogers Clark in his expedition against Vincennes. They were friendly and helpful to the early settlers. However, the primary reason for naming the chapter after the Piankeshaws was that the tract known as "Clark's Grant" was ceded to Colonel Clark by the Piankeshaws before it was given to him by the government. This deed of gift was uniquely embodied in the following:

Declaration:

Whereas, for many years past this once peaceable land hath been put in confusion by the English encouraging all people to raise the tomahawk against the big knives, saying they were bad people, rebellious, and ought to be put from under the sun and their names be no more.

But as the sky of our councils was always misty and never clear, we still were at a loss to know what to do, hoping that the Master of Life would, one day or other, make the sky clear and put us in the right road. He taking pity on us, sent a father among us (Col. Clark) who has cleared our eyes and made our paths straight, defending our lands, etc., so that we now enjoy peace from the rising to the setting of the sun, and the nations even to the heads of the great river, (Mississippi) are happy and will not more listen to bad birds, but abide by the councils of their great father, a chief of the big knives that is now among us.

And, whereas, it is our desire that he should long remain among us that we may take his counsel and be happy; it being also our desire to give him lands to reside on in our country, that we may at all times speak to him, after many solicitations to him to make a choice of a tract, he choosing the lands adjoining the falls of the Ohio, on the west side of the river.

I do hereby, in the name of all the great chiefs and warriors of the Wabash and their allies, declare that so much land at the falls of the Ohio, contained in said bounds

To-wit: Beginning opposite the middle of the first island below the falls, bounded upwards by the west bank of the river so as to include two leagues and a half on a straight line from the beginning; thence at right angles with said line two leagues and a half in breadth in all its parts, shall hereafter and ever be the sole property of our great father (Col. Clark) with all things thereto belonging, either above or below the earth, shall be and is his, except a road through said land to his door, which shall remain ours, and for us to walk on to speak to our father. All nations from the rising to the setting of the sun, who are not in alliance with us, are hereby warned to esteem said gift as sacred and not to make that land taste of blood; that all people either at peace or war may repair in safety to get counsel of our father. Whoever first darken that land shall no longer have a name. This declaration shall forever be a witness between all actions and our present great father; that said lands are forever hereafter his property.

In witness whereof, I do, in the name of all great chiefs and warriors of the Wabash, in open council, affix my mark and seal, done at St. Vincent, this 16th day of June 1779.
(Signed) Francis, Son of Tobacco[22]

In the very early years of Piankeshaw Chapter, Mrs. Frances Rice Maginness proposed, and it was unanimously adopted, that the chapter flower be the columbine because of the following emblematic description:

It grows wild in every state of the union, from the Atlantic to the Pacific, and from Canada to the Gulf, with the exception of a very small region about the mouth of the Mississippi but even there can be grown from the seed. The flower's very name suggests our beloved Columbia. The botanical name of the flower—Aquiligia—was given to it for the reason that the flower when reversed resembles an eagle's talons. Nor is this all the symbolism we can trace in the flower. A front view suggests the outline of a beautiful five-rayed star, and a single petal in the shape of a horn of plenty; among different colors, there are the brilliant red, pure white and blue, our national colors, and the further significant fact is that the leaf of the Columbine being made up of many segments, exemplifies our motto "E Pluribus Unum." [23]

MARY CARDWILL, FOUNDING REGENT

Membership of the New Albany Piankeshaw Chapter of the DAR contains a long list of many notable women. One, however, stands out above the rest. It is important to record a brief biography of Mary Cardwill since she was the founding regent of this chapter in 1898.

Miss Cardwill, who, when only fifteen years old, was a licensed teacher, contributed to newspapers such as the *Louisville Courier Journal*, the *Indianapolis Journal* and to various magazines including the *Ladies Home Journal* and the *Shakesperiana*. With Maurice Thompson, James Whitcomb Riley and others, she was a member of the Western Association of Writers founded in Indianapolis. Following the Nineteenth Amendment, she, by invitation, cast the first feminine vote in New Albany.

She was named chairman of the Women's Auxiliary of the committee that planned the celebration of New Albany's centennial in 1913. Following this, she organized the present New Albany Women's Club and was a charter member of the Altrusa Club. She was also instrumental in founding the New Albany Public Library. For fifteen years, she served as attendance officer in New Albany and was the first woman to be appointed to the police department in the city, though she was not a salaried member of the police force.

Mary was the daughter of John Cardwill and sister of Judge George B. Cardwill, who is credited with being the first person to advocate a telephone system for New Albany. She died in November 1937 at the age of eighty-four.

Mary Cardwill. *Courtesy Indiana History Room, New Albany–Floyd County Public Library.*

Purchase of the Scribner House

The suggestion to purchase the Scribner House occurred at a meeting held on September 9, 1916. At first the chairman of the Monument Committee suggested the chapter place a marker in a conspicuous place as a memorial to the Scribners. Mrs. Burnham of Bedford then brought up the idea of purchasing the house, and the idea received much enthusiasm. Miss Hattie, who made her living by teaching piano lessons, was still living in the house at that time. She was also enthusiastic about the idea and said she would sell the house for $1,500. Following much discussion, a motion was made in November 1916 to purchase the Scribner House using, in part, the money the women had saved for the Scribner memorial monument. By May 1917, through savings and loans, there was enough money to purchase it. On September 8, 1917, the daughters met in their new home. On September 20, 1917, only twelve days later and before another meeting, Miss Hattie was called to her heavenly home.

The goal of the chapter was to hold a "burning of the mortgage" event on Flag Day in 1928. The chapter minutes from the event read, "Candles were lighted and things were in readiness for the burning, when a sentimental mood possessed those present, and then and there they decided to keep the notes for preservation. Great happiness prevailed but serious thoughts were in order, too, for now the restoration would begin."

Scribner House, as it appeared when the DAR purchased it. Note the long windows. *Courtesy Piankeshaw Chapter DAR.*

RESTORATION AND CARE OF THE SCRIBNER HOUSE

For more than ninety-five years, the focus of the DAR has been to maintain Scribner House. This book can only summarize the struggles of the chapter to preserve and maintain this historic treasure. Piankeshaw Chapter has been uniquely fortunate to have this trust and to keep the house in shape for visitors who come to see it.

Photographs of the Scribner House at the time of the centennial celebration in 1913 indicate that it was in need of paint and other repairs. Not until 1928, when the debt on the house was retired, could the chapter turn attention to raising money for restoration needed. Card parties, silver and colonial teas, auctions, ice cream socials and rummage sales were held. A concert netted about $300. There were many public donations.

In 1932, during the term of Miss Lillian Emery as regent, major work on the house was undertaken. Dr. William Augustus Scribner, second owner of the house, had lengthened the front parlor windows in the New Orleans style, ceiling-to-floor. During the restoration work, the parlor windows were restored to their shorter length to conform with windows in the rest of the house, as in the earliest photo, circa 1850. The chimneys were repaired and a new roof installed. The porches were ready to collapse, so the floors and posts were replaced. Some of the exterior siding was replaced and the house painted again. At that time, there were occasional rag rugs in use, and members waxed the floors from time to time, but they often splintered.

Termites had eaten away the wooden floor supports of the family kitchen, and the floorboards had collapsed onto the ground. Dissension arose in the chapter as to whether to replace the wood floor or put in a brick floor. To settle the matter, a concrete floor was poured with the idea that a wooden floor could be installed on top of it later. In January 1933, the house committee reported the total cost of restoration as $1,746.71, plus $40.00 for upholstering furniture.

Soon after World War II, the chapter borrowed $800 from Mrs. Durbin, a member whose family had helped to organize the chapter in 1898. It was necessary to replace a large part of the weather boarding on the west side of the house, replace windowsills and again repaint the house. The only member financially able to be of such help, she would not allow her name to be mentioned in connection with the interest-free loan, which the chapter paid off a little at a time.

On September 22, 1947, an important step was taken toward establishing a permanent income. It was decided to have a Scribner House plate made

View of Scribner House in the early 1930s. Note the shortened windows. *Courtesy Piankeshaw Chapter DAR.*

for sale to the public. Eight members advanced a loan of $725 to the chapter to begin the project. After a design for the plate was finally accepted by the artist for the manufacturer, Jones McDuffee & Stratton of Boston, Massachusetts, a contract was signed on May 14, 1948. The first order of six hundred plates was received May 23, 1950. Sales were so good that a second order for fifty dozen was sent on May 23, 1951, and cups and saucers were ordered to match the plates. All proceeds were allocated for repairs to the Scribner House. Proceeds from sales to that time, after repayment of the loan, were $362.91. The sample plate was framed and now hangs in the parlor of the house. In 1963, plates were still being sold during the sesquicentennial celebration. Scribner House was open to the public on Thursday, Friday and Saturday evenings, with members welcoming guests during the historic festivities.

In order to raise funds to support upkeep of Scribner House, many ideas were put into action, such as annual "Bring-and-Buy" sales. Sometimes antiques were contributed for sale. For many meetings, an assigned member brought a cake for auction to members. Rummage sales were frequent, and for a while, a thrift shop was operated from the cottage. Chances were sold on donated quilts, displayed in a local bank. Sometimes individual members were able to help by donating monetary gifts or loaning interest-free funds for major repairs, such as to the roof, to the porches, for necessary rewiring and for installation of plumbing.

In the early 1950s, the present little kitchen on the south side of the lower level was created for the use of the chapter, since the space for storage of wood and coal was no longer needed. The first addition was the sink and a hot water heater. The faucet was on the outside and always needed to be cut off before the temperature dropped below freezing. A two-burner electric heater was used to make coffee. By 1959, the porches were again in need of repair. The cost this time was $157.17. A garden party was planned with coffee and rolls in the morning and sandwiches and lemonade in the afternoon. Tickets were $1.00 per person. Apparently, these were also card parties because there was a notation that members were directed to bring their own card tables. This fundraiser was repeated for several years. During this time, the house was open to the public one day in each of the following months: September, October, November, April, May and June.

By 1963, it became necessary to make a major decision regarding the care and maintenance of Scribner House. Major repairs were a constant responsibility and therefore the chapter felt it had to reach out to the community for support. Lillian Emery had netted the chapter $450 by speaking before groups interested in preserving the house for posterity. Community leaders came forward with an offer to transfer the care, control and management of the Scribner House to the New Albany City Parks and Recreation Board. The matter was presented to the chapter and referred to the DAR board for further investigation. The advantages, as well as disadvantages, were thoughtfully and carefully considered. The board voted unanimously against this conveyance of title to outside parties. At the January 10, 1963 meeting, members confirmed this action. It was resolved that the title and ownership of the valuable DAR property in New Albany should be held by the local Piankeshaw Chapter at any cost and not turned over to the national organization, another chapter or an outside third party to operate, though the regent expressed appreciation for the interest displayed by the parks department and by those in the community who offered to help.

In April 1964, investigations were made through Historic New Albany concerning the property immediately west of the Scribner House. It was found that the Spur Oil Company, which owned the lot, would be willing to sell. Their original price was too high, but further negotiations reduced the price, with the chapter agreeing to remove any and all buildings and plant the lot in shrubbery and trees. In October 1964, the property was bought by Pauline Strack and her husband and presented to the chapter as a memorial to Pauline's mother, Aurelia Rowland Hickey, a former chapter regent. After that purchase, members donated $600 for the purchase of the back half of that lot. The old block building left by the oil company was removed, and through the summer of 1965, members worked to clean up the lot. Debris was removed and large holes filled with dirt and sod.

During that same year, members met almost weekly to work on making the beautiful braided wool rugs that still grace all floors of the house. Used wool clothing was contributed by members. It is said that some husbands feared their wives would take their favored clothing for the purpose and so took them to work. By April 1966, two beautiful rugs had been completed. A year later, a large rug three yards in diameter was completed, and more rugs had been started. In October 1968, it was announced that nineteen members had spent 2,010 hours at the Scribner House braiding the rugs. In addition, many hours were spent at their homes washing, coloring, cutting and pressing the woolen material. The work on the rugs continued for several years, into the 1970s.

A large tree had to be removed from the property to the east of Scribner House. A huge limb had fallen and severely damaged the east side of the caretaker's cottage, along with its siding, roof and guttering. There followed a long battle to force payment from the proprietor next door. Finally, he agreed to pay, but the chapter bore the expense of replacing studs that had rotted. That work was accomplished in 1965, but other repairs to the house and cottage, long delayed, became urgent. After considerable discussion, the chapter passed an amendment in September 1966 changing the bylaws to provide that, for a period of five years, members would pay a special fee per

The filling station built on the west side of Scribner House that replaced the earlier Scribner & Maginess Drug Store. *Courtesy Barbara Whiteside.*

Scribner House garden after cleanup of the west corner lot. *Photo by Anne Caudill.*

annum to create a fund to take care of necessary repairs to Scribner House property. In case this should work a hardship on a member, payment of the special fee could be waived. It was reported that nonresident members were also responsive to this assessment. Thus, the support of the house was more broadly shared. (In 1968, this was made a standing rule and deleted from the bylaws.) Again, as a result, safe and adequate wiring for the house and cottage was accomplished and properly certified. A new coat of white paint gave the house a face-lift. A new front fence was painted by DAR members. The ceilings on the first and second floors were in urgent need of renewal, as they were peeling badly. The roof of the cottage needed repainting. New curtains were purchased for the downstairs hall and the two rooms on the ground floor. With the cost of these repairs in mind, it was decided in May 1967 to charge admission of fifty cents to tour Scribner House. Exception would be made for schoolchildren, whose fees were taken care of by the New Albany–Floyd County Consolidated School Corporation.

During that same time, the chapter decided on a new fundraising event. The members and guests brought items to be auctioned to the November meeting. The auctioneer gave a new interpretation of "DAR" with a sign bearing the words "DARING-AUCTION-RIVALRY."

Wynema Wagoner, former regent, recalled that it was about 1968 that the chapter decided not to rent the cottage any more and to use it as an office. The glass-fronted cabinet was moved to the cottage from the basement storage room of the main house and a new base cabinet built to hold it. The gift shop in the front room of the cottage was organized and opened to tours.

In 1969, the chapter librarian requested that a thirteen- by sixteen-inch deed be framed and hold a place of honor in the Scribner House. The framed original deed is for Lot #15 on lower Third Street in New Albany (Clark County at that time), Indiana, dated November 26, 1817, and signed by Scribner brothers Joel, Nathaniel and Abner and their wives. The lot was sold to Sylvester Perry, and the deed was recorded May 1818.

By 1969, it became an urgent matter to replace the Scribner House roof, and a bid for $275 was accepted. The project was delayed until June, when the chapter would be in a better position to meet this financial obligation. A rummage sale was planned to raise funds. Looking to the future, some of the other essentials needed were the addition of a restroom, beautifying the garden and furnishing the front bedroom.

A committee was appointed by the regent to select wallpaper for the three rooms on the second floor. The necessity for repapering was found when Mr. Melheiser did the ceilings and discovered that the side walls were in bad

Deed signed by Scribner brothers and their wives on November 26, 1817. *Courtesy Piankeshaw Chapter DAR.*

condition. The committee consisted of Mrs. William Durbin, Mrs. Maybelle Collins and Mrs. Arthur Payne. Following is the list of work accomplished during the summer months by this committee, with the help of the regent. The volunteer work done by chapter members is typical of the work done every year to maintain Scribner House.

1. Wallpaper was purchased at Reinhart's at half price. Due to the beauty and quality of the paper, the committee felt the need for a complete re-decorating of the second floor. Mrs. Reinhart gave a gallon of Porter's semi-gloss enamel, one quart of undercoat and sandpaper. All woodwork was washed, sanded, all holes filled and woodwork painted.

2. All washable items in the two display cases were washed by hand. All wool items were dry cleaned by Star Cleaners at no charge, courtesy of Mrs. Elmer Ehalt.

3. All silver services were polished. One teapot, badly bent at the base, and a tall brass Colonial candlestick were repaired by E.&E. Jewelers, located next door to Scribner House.
4. All brass candlesticks in the house were polished.
5. All window shades on the first and second floors were washed.
6. The applique quilt used on the poster bed was cleaned by Star Cleaners at no charge. The canopy and bed ruffles were laundered by a committee member.
7. Curtains from the first floor were washed, ironed and placed at the second-floor windows.
8. Curtain rods were replaced at all windows on the first and second floors. These were purchased at Grant's at 10 percent discount given by manager Les Kerr.
9. Linoleum on the floor of the display cabinet in the front room on the second floor was painted. Walls of this cabinet were papered by a committee member.
10. The Seth Thomas clock in the back bedroom was refinished and restored by a committee member.
11. The looking glass was restored.
12. The wallpaper in the upstairs hall was cleaned by the committee. All woodwork in the hall was washed and windows repainted.
13. A leak in the cornice over the front of the house was repaired by R.A. Huncilman & Co. They also sealed some small cracks that may have been the cause of the damp plaster under these windows. This wall was then treated with a damp-resistant paint before the repapering.
14. Wallpaper was cleaned in the hall and two rooms on the first floor. Also, window woodwork was sanded and washed, holes filled and two coats of paint applied. All windows were washed. General house cleaning was done by chapter members.
15. Three rooms on the second floor were papered by Mr. Melheiser.

The members who had been working diligently to paint, paper and decorate the downstairs dining room completed their work, and a vinyl floor covering in a random plank pattern was installed over the concrete floor. That cost was $397. The expenses of these recent renovations were paid for from the interest accumulated in the Scribner House Memorial (Endowment) Fund. Its $5,000 certificate of deposite (CD) yielded about $400 yearly to be used for the maintenance of the house.

The next year, plans to install a lavatory in the house went forward even though some members thought the old outhouse was sufficient. The only available sewer for a tie-in had been installed earlier from the brick building next door. After considerable negotiation, the owner of that building agreed to allow the digging for the installation of a line to tie into the sewer line. In addition to the cost of labor and rental of equipment, it was necessary to pay a $300.00 "tap-in" fee to the city council. The plumber agreed to payment of $441.67 in four installments over four years. Eventually, however, it became necessary to replace the tap-in line with a separate one.

Very large water bills were noted in January 1976 due to a water leak. The leak was found, and the hydrant in the yard was fixed so that it could not be turned on from outside the house. A no-smoking ban was enacted by the chapter in March 1976. In April, it was reported the porches had been repaired again, this time at a cost of $934.17.

Scribner House was placed on the National Register of Historic Places in December 1977 by the United States Department of Natural Resources. The plaque noting this honor was later registered in the county recorder's office. Soon after that, the Floyd County Historical Society proposed to erect a historical plaque commemorating the Scribner brothers as founders of New Albany. The offer was accepted by the chapter in 1979. A plaque was installed on the corner of State and Main Streets set in concrete and surrounded by short metal posts, a chain and appropriate shrubs.

In 1980, several members donated electric logs. These made the parlors much more cheerful during the winter months and continue to be used since actual wood fires are no longer needed or convenient. By September 1980, necessary rewiring of the house had been completed at a cost of $2,640.00. Chances on a donated quilt made by a member brought $518.75, and two members made loans to the chapter totaling $1,500.00, without interest. The skilled needleworker was at work on another quilt to be offered for sale by chances.

In 1981, there was concern as to the security of the house. It was decided to put a solid wooden door at the rear entrance and a deadbolt lock on the front door. It was suggested that bars be put on the windows, but this was not undertaken.

During this time, there were other improvements made to the house. A cap was placed on the chimney, and insulation was added to the sidewalls of the third-floor nursery, funded through a member's pledge of $130. The thermostat was moved from the front hall to the inside wall of the front parlor. These improvements were made to cut down on heating costs. A rummage sale netted $33, and chances sold on a quilt made by a member brought in $717. The installation of an air conditioner was completed in October 1982. The painting of the west side of the exterior of the house (at the most reasonable bid) was authorized. In 1984, a broken water line on the side of the house was discovered. It cost $328 to install a new line and two outside water spigots. The next need was replacement of the second-floor hall ceiling that was ready to fall.

In 1985, a letter written in 1955 by Mary Scribner to Alice Greene was brought to the attention of the chapter. It listed various furnishings that were in the Scribner House as late as 1955. A number of listed items could no longer be found in the house, and there was no record of their disposal. The chapter felt it necessary to do a complete inventory. A committee was established to oversee furnishings and to make decisions on all donated items as to their relevance to the house and its period. The committee consisted of all past regents in good standing and six members elected by the chapter (two each year) for six-year terms. The chapter also approved a motion that, effective September 10, 1987, it would no longer accept any furniture or materials on loan to be placed in Scribner House.

In 1987, part of the clapboards on the house were removed to reveal the post and beam interior construction filled with stacks of culled, soft brick piled on planks and held together with clay. This was a cheap but effective way to insulate the house and allow for interior plastering to be placed directly over the brick without using laths to support the plaster. It was also discovered that the house framework was fastened with wooden pegs and square nails.

By 1988, heating and air-conditioning had been installed in the cottage but not in the upstairs rooms of Scribner House itself. Therefore, in October the chapter had heating and air-conditioning for the two upper floors put in. It had become necessary for the preservation of artifacts in the house.

In the early 1980s, the portrait of William Augustus Scribner, which hangs in the front parlor and is so important for the house, had shown signs of deterioration. By June 1982, it had been "restored" and was back on the wall under glass. The charge was $25 for the cost of the glass only. But by 1990, it was clear that the portrait had suffered serious damage due to the paint adhering to the glass. The chapter was faced with raising $7,000 for the restoration of the portrait. Because of the serious nature of the deterioration, it was decided to hire a professional to clean and restore it. In December 1990, the portrait of Dr. Scribner was hand-carried by a representative of the Speed Art Museum in Louisville to McKay Lodge Fine Arts in Cincinnati, Ohio, for a written estimate of the cost of removing the

Exposed post and beam construction of the Scribner House. *Photo by Anne Caudill. Courtesy Piankeshaw Chapter DAR.*

glass and restoring the badly deteriorated painting. Value of the portrait was estimated at $5,000. A committee was formed and sent out letters requesting help, first to chapter members, then to Scribner family descendants. By April 1992, the portrait of William Augustus Scribner was again hanging in the front parlor. The placement of glass covering the painting was necessary due to the heavy oil reconstruction of the portrait. But this time, spacers were placed between the glass and the portrait, and it was hermetically sealed.

Four gaslights were donated to be used on the lawn. For many years, several donors have given large gifts to the chapter to be used for maintenance of the house. These bequests continue to be of great assistance.

During the summer of 1990, a list of much-needed improvements and repairs for the house was drawn up: the furnace and air conditioner needed servicing, and the air conditioner of the third floor needed to be replaced; a hot water heater was needed for the kitchen; vines on the house had to be removed; and repair to the drain at the front corner of the house was a priority. The house was in need of a thorough cleaning. Once again it was decided to approach some local businesses, organizations and individuals for ongoing annual contributions to Scribner House upkeep. Letters requesting funds were sent out in February 1991.

The brick sidewalks were rebuilt in 1996–99, with the assistance of the Kiwanis Club and as an Eagle Scout project.

With the start of a new decade in 2000, a wooden floor was finally installed over the concrete floor in the old kitchen. New storm doors, wooden fencing, a new rose arbor, rug pads, resilvering of the front door plate, new wallpaper in the parlors and replacement of the posts and flooring on the porch were all accomplished. A video and audio system was also installed. A new furnace, air conditioner, refrigerator and refinements to the kitchen shelving were all done and made the house more convenient and comfortable. Painting of the storage room, waterproofing of the front foundation walls and various small repairs have come about through gifts, grants and much volunteer labor from the husband of the regent.

A special effort during this decade was made to increase the endowment fund. This fund is set aside for major catastrophic needs, and it is anticipated that the interest from it will be used for the annual maintenance costs, thus easing the need to raise funds from the community each year. The support of the community through large and small gifts has made it possible to keep Scribner House available as a museum of the history of New Albany.

In 2004, the old square piano was returned beautifully repaired and restored in time for use at the Christmas Tea. Gifts from the community of $4,000 were matched by Caesar's Foundation to cover the $8,000 cost of restoration.

The sale of Kroger gift cards to members was begun. Through this program, the chapter receives 4 percent of every $100 spent at Krogers by members, and each year it has brought in helpful amounts. Proceeds from the gift shop increased due to creative buying. For example, it was decided to commission the manufacture of souvenir pottery pitchers in preparation for the upcoming 1813 bicentennial celebration of the founding of New Albany. The handsome, hand-turned pitchers are glazed in grey and bear a sketch of Scribner House in blue surrounded by the words "Scribner House Est. 1814." The pitchers are 6.5 inches high and hold a quart of liquid.

In October 2004, the New Albany mayor met with the chapter to discuss concerns about the extensive building project of the YMCA across the street, especially with regard to the large number of adults and children who would be crossing our historic site. It was expected the project would require two-and-a-half years to complete. He discussed the locations of the building, natatorium, parking spaces and other potential buildings in the city's plans. He explained that the block of State Street along the side of Scribner House would be closed to parking and traffic during construction. He assured the chapter that no blasting was planned and that there would be special parking privileges for members at times needed to facilitate chapter activities and for aid to members who needed care in walking. He explained that a security fence would be installed to protect our property during construction. A small building was razed on the YMCA property that bore an official Corps of Engineers demarcation of the flood level of 1937. That sign was reinstalled in the front hallway of Scribner House at the same level to show how high the waters reached during that flood.

Major changes came to the neighborhood during the next few years as the YMCA took shape. The property between Scribner House and the flood wall was cleared by the city of its small old commercial buildings and used for the staging of supplies and equipment for the construction project. That area eventually became a city parking lot. Major excavations on the YMCA lot necessitated the closing of traffic on that section of State Street. The chapter was forewarned of the driving of piles necessary to support the new building, with vibrations of the earth resulting. In December 2006, all the portraits and other framed pictures and documents were removed from Scribner House walls. Delicate historic glass and china was carefully packed to prevent possible damage from the pile driving, which continued for many weeks.

The huge old poplar tree in the front yard of the house became a matter of concern. Large limbs were dying from disease, posing a risk to the children and others who passed beneath it as they entered the house. With the advice of the USDA agricultural agent, an arborist was employed to treat and prune the diseased limbs. This was a major expense, but the disease was arrested, due in part to consistent watering during a very dry summer.

By 2006, it was discovered that the rear porches, repaired four years earlier, had not been properly done and were dangerously deteriorated. It was necessary to completely redo them at a cost of $11,584, covered by a grant from Community Foundation of Southern Indiana. The work was undertaken by Traditional American Builders, workmen skilled in historic preservation. The next restoration undertaken was replacement of the crumbling brick wall on the exterior of the little kitchen and lavatory. That expense was covered partly by gifts from the community and members and partly by chapter savings.

At the request of the chapter, a preliminary survey of the need for restoration work on Scribner House was done in order to ensure its continuation for another two hundred years. The survey was done with the consultation and close oversight of the regent's husband. The survey found that the most pressing problem was the wooden sills, which were seriously rotted. The west wall of the house had pulled away from the staircase. The old clapboard siding, many times repainted and patched, needed to be replaced and the window framing taken apart and rebuilt along with roof, gutter and downspout replacement. All old electrical wiring needed to be updated to meet current electrical code specifications. There were areas where wallpaper and old plaster needed to be replaced, fireplaces and chimneys inspected and repaired and interior woodwork repainted. When all was said and done, the architectural study showed an estimated cost of necessary renovations amounted to approximately $521,112. The detailed assessment was used for grant applications.

There was much discussion as to other ways to raise the money needed for the restoration. The consensus was that the work would have to be accomplished in phases and that the chapter would make sure there was enough financing available for each phase. All members were to be kept informed and involved in the progress and cost of the huge project.

On May 4, 2008, a new approach to fundraising efforts was staged: an "Antiques Appraisal Fair." It was held on the lawn of Scribner House in a large tent, under the guidance of a widely known and respected auctioneer and an additional appraiser. It was a perfect spring day, and a large number of people brought items to be appraised. The additional lure of a silent auction of items donated by members and many businesses made it a great success, both socially and financially. The antiques appraisal and silent auction fundraiser was held again in 2009 at the YMCA building.

In October 2009, after months of discussion and planning, the chapter voted to allow the Horseshoe Foundation to develop the Scribner House garden into a small urban park that would symbolize the downtown redevelopment and beautification effort. The completed Scribner Garden was dedicated on May 2, 2010. It featured a graceful bronze sculpture that was dedicated on December 5, 2010, at the time of the annual Scribner House Christmas Tea and open house. The sculpture includes four open books with text addressing the Scribner family's impact on New Albany: the founding of New Albany; the Scribner House; leadership for a young settlement; and education and religion. For the chapter, this 2010 dedication was a reaffirmation of the careful nurturing begun years ago and continued by the DAR through the years.

The park is living up to every expectation and perhaps exceeding the wildest dreams. It is enjoyed daily by New Albany citizens and visitors who find a lovely oasis in the midst of busy modern lives. Scribner House was

Scribner House Garden as it appears in 2012. *Photo by Curt Peters.*

Garden sculpture dedicated to the Scribner family. *Photo by K. Holwerk.*

Newest neighbor to Scribner House—the YMCA. *Photo by Curt Peters.*

once again the focal point of New Albany when the mayor chose this garden as the site for his inauguration on December 20, 2011. The oldest standing structure in the city is vital to the daily life of today's New Albany.

The Caretakers Who Lived in the Cottage (1932–1961)

In 1932, in the interest of caring for the Scribner House, the DAR chapter decided to arrange for caretakers to live in the cottage behind the house. This cottage, built around 1850, had been Dr. William A. Scribner's medical office and later served as a summer kitchen. When the DAR bought the property, there was a large cookstove in the front room, and the back room was used as a bedroom. Soon the DAR rented the cottage to a family as caretakers. In an article from the *New Albany Tribune* on May 4, 2003, Mr. William Ferguson, then age seventy-one, told of spending his early years there with his father, Walter Ferguson, and his mother, Georgia Foster Ferguson. Walter was employed at Connor Manufacturing in Louisville. Two more children were born to the Fergusons while they lived in the cottage: Doris, born in 1934, and Bobby, born in 1939.

The Fergusons took care of the house, the lawn and gardens. William related how, before each DAR meeting, the whole house was swept, dusted and polished. His father took care of the fireplaces that heated the house. His mother made tea or coffee to accompany the refreshments the DAR ladies brought for the meetings. Little William looked forward to the leftover cookies, mints and other goodies that the family received. He enjoyed the meeting days when the ladies came in their pretty dresses. While the house was readied, he could visit there. He was awed by the portraits and fine furnishings. He played in the yard and delighted in observing the passing scene on Main Street or on the river and its banks. He tells that there was a railway passenger station between the house and the river, of much interest to watch.

By 1939, their family had grown too large for the cottage, so the Fergusons moved to a larger home a few blocks away. At that time, Georgia Ferguson's parents, Mr. and Mrs. Foster, took over as caretakers, living there for about fifteen years. When ill health made it impossible for them to care for the property, they moved away.[24]

On September 11, 1958, the chapter minutes note that Dawn Condra, a DAR member, was the new resident of the cottage and that "...the Scribner

Cottage located behind Scribner House. *Photo by Curt Peters.*

House looked lovely and pristine under her care." In May 1961, chapter minutes noted there were expenditures for cleaning the house and carrying firewood. By November 1961, the chapter had to find a replacement as Miss Condra was in the hospital and did not plan to resume duties as the resident caretaker. The duties of cleaning were then supervised for a time by a chapter member.

Duties of the Caretakers of Scribner House
By the Board of Directors, November 14, 1941

House shall be dusted and in perfect order and fires built when necessary for our Chapter meetings.

House shall be thoroughly cleaned once a year, in April, window and woodwork washed, etc.

Curtains shall be taken down after the November meeting and not put up again until the April meeting. They shall be washed carefully and put away during winter months and left rough-dry without being starched. Chapter will furnish soap for laundering curtains, also floor wax and furniture polish used in the house.

House shall be open to public inspection upon payment of ten-cent fee per person. The fees are to be the property of caretaker.

Guests visiting house are to sign Guest Book.

Fees of 25 cents from the sale of Scribner House Book are to be turned over to Mrs. May Conner, Treasurer.

Members may show the house to their own personal guests free of charge at any time.

Caretaker shall have use of the two-room cottage on rear of lot, rent-free. Also, he shall have the use of the little kitchen in the basement of Scribner House but not the big kitchen.

Caretaker shall assume responsibility for payment of all utilities (water $1.00 a month minimum), electricity ($1.50 a month minimum), except when lights are used in Scribner House for which the Chapter will make reasonable payment.

Yards and walks shall be properly taken care of at all times of the year by caretaker.

Caretaker shall be responsible for turning off water in winter weather in hydrant in yard.

Caretaker must keep house carefully locked at all times when not displaying it to guests.

Mildred Rogers Hartman
Regent, Piankeshaw Chapter DAR

The Flood of 1937

In January 1937, the most devastating flood of the Ohio River recorded to date was a major disaster. The building of the flood walls afterward were the response of the federal government to prevent another such occurrence. There was an amusing incident following the flood when someone, in searching through damaged papers, found an old handbill that had been printed by the Scribner brothers on July 16, 1813. The handbill listed the city's advantages, according to the Scribner brothers' viewpoint, and cited the following: "The bank adjoining the river is high and not subject to inundation."

The flood brought water into the cottage as well as into the Scribner House kitchen and up into the parlors above. All furnishings were moved to upper floors except the jam and jelly cupboard in the kitchen and the 1858 Steinway square piano in the parlor, which could not be moved up the narrow stairway. Wynema Wagoner recalled hearing members Elizabeth Payne and Maybelle Collins tell of scraping mud from the piano legs so that they could be revarnished.

Minutes of Piankeshaw Chapter record that, because of the high water in the house and the aftermath of necessary repairs, chapter meetings were held in private homes from February until October 1937. It is recorded that when danger of flooding appeared imminent, Mrs. Anderson, the regent, and Mrs. Strack went to the house and gave Mr. Ferguson, the caretaker, permission to store his own furniture in Scribner House. They asked him to move DAR furniture upstairs as needed. They also gave their approval for him to stay in the main house for his convenience and for protection against looting.

In March 1937, the ladies estimated it would cost $400.00 to repair Scribner House after the flood damage. They reported this loss to the Red Cross. However, in the end, the Red Cross did not have funds to assist institutions. The list included $25.00 for repair of the piano and $15.00 for repair of a sideboard. The loss on the cottage was estimated at $150.00. The chapter felt that repairing the cottage for Mr. Ferguson was a priority. By the May meeting, the cottage had been painted. In July, bids for the repair work for both buildings show a total of $208.00. Mr. Hatton donated the work he did cleaning and restoring the floors, and other workmen reduced their bids. In order to raise the money necessary, it was decided to write to each member and ask that they make a voluntary donation for the work. By October, $195.75 had been received for the rehabilitation and there were pledges amounting to $40.00. The work included refinishing floors, painting woodwork, papering the walls, repairing hearths and cleaning rugs. In September, it was decided to wait until the following spring to refinish the lower level of Scribner House on account of the dampness of the beams and the need for exterminating termites. The ceiling was stained and had so much mud dried on it that they decided to cover it with wallboard. A rummage sale to raise funds was planned, and this became an annual event held for many years.

On October 9, 1937, Piankeshaw Chapter held its thirty-ninth anniversary meeting in the Scribner House. The minutes stated, "The Old House looked as though it had taken great pains to prepare for a birthday party. The floors, woodwork, wallpaper, furniture and rugs had all been renewed. It seemed fitting that our first meeting in the house after the flood should be an anniversary meeting. Miss Cardwill, founding Regent, was to have been a hostess, but was too ill to attend."

ADDITIONAL PROJECTS AND ACTIVITIES OF PIANKESHAW CHAPTER DAR

The minutes of the chapter from its beginning in 1898 until the present are voluminous and detailed. Through the years, the membership has carried forward the objectives of the National DAR organization in many ways. The preservation of historic Scribner House is only one of the many activities that have occupied the attention, skills, time and finances of the members. This book can only summarize the history of the Scribner family and its influence on the town they founded and the struggles of Piankeshaw Chapter to preserve and maintain this historic treasure. Piankeshaw Chapter has been uniquely fortunate to have this trust. From 1813 to 1951, six generations of the Scribner family lived in New Albany. In fact, on July 8, 1951, Harriet Scribner, great-great-great-granddaughter of Joel Scribner and great-great-granddaughter of Dr. William Augustus Scribner, was married to Richard Morris Pennington Jr. Mary Flowers, a DAR member, served a wedding breakfast in the Scribner House dining room for the bride and groom and immediate family members. Certainly, no other place could have been so appropriately chosen as a part of that important day for Harriet Scribner, sixth generation of the Scribner family.

Special days too numerous to mention have been observed. The golden anniversary of the chapter (1948–49) was remembered as a special time. Many came to the October meeting in colonial costumes. Rereading of fifty-year-old minutes and reminiscing by past regents was featured. A special luncheon was served at the Legion Home with past regents serving as hostesses. Ninety-three members, guests and state officers were present at the celebration.

The chapter has always been involved in community activities. We can only name a few. The first project adopted by Piankeshaw Chapter was to locate unmarked graves of Revolutionary War soldiers in Floyd, Harrison, Crawford, Washington, Scott and Orange Counties. The federal government had promised to provide marble markers such as those for veterans of the Civil War. After a long and tedious search, a total of thirty graves were identified. Five of the graves were located in New Albany's Fairview Cemetery and two in rural Floyd County. A major project was started in

Memorial to veterans of the American Revolution located in Veterans Plaza on Market Street. *Photo by Curt Peters.*

the very earliest years to raise funds for placing a memorial on the Veterans Plaza in memory of those Revolutionary soldiers buried in Floyd County. Mary Cardwill and Helen Fawcett worked diligently to plan and carry out this project. Another example of community service was the chapter's 1902 involvement in getting a bill passed to erect a monument to the victims of the Pigeon Roost Massacre in Scott County. In 1913, Piankeshaw Chapter participated in New Albany's centennial celebration with a float in the parade depicting George Rogers Clark receiving the deed to the grant of land from the Son of Tobacco.

For many years, members of the chapter attended a church service in a body during the month of February to commemorate the birthdays of Washington and Lincoln. During World War I, the daughters were engaged in making shirts for the soldiers. Many bought yarn and knitted for the Red Cross. They contributed to a Belgian Fund and, in 1918, adopted a French orphan for two years. They contributed to National DAR projects to build a hospital and water systems and provided ambulances in France. After World War I, they celebrated Arbor Day by planting an evergreen tree at the plaza on Market Street to honor the men who served in that war.

In 1937, Mrs. Siebolt presented a chapter banner as a gift. She and Elisabeth Payne, her daughter, embroidered the beautiful DAR insignia. It remains a chapter treasure.

It was noted that there was no marker of any kind at the grave of Mrs. Annabelle Smith Hartley, a founding member. By unanimous vote, it was agreed that a marker be placed in appreciation for all Mrs. Hartley had done for the chapter. As the first organization meeting of the chapter had been held in her home, it seemed appropriate that the marker should be placed on that same date—October 15, 1937.

During World War II, members again gave of their time and means. Among other things, members donated many hours toward the sale of defense bonds amounting to several thousand dollars. In 1946, a citation was received from the U.S. Treasury Department for services rendered in the war finance program. Their answer to the appeals for scrap metal during that war served two purposes. Not only did they gather together much-needed materials for the war effort, but they added forty dollars to their general fund by selling scrap and junk.

Regular meetings of Piankeshaw DAR are held in the upstairs parlors of the house. Patriotic subjects, history, national concerns, art and matters of local concern are discussed. After the business is taken care of and interesting programs presented, the members adjourn to the downstairs dining room, where the hostesses of the month serve delicious desserts and tea, coffee or punch from a table beautifully decorated in a seasonal motif. The old room again glows with the conviviality it knew from its beginning. Sometimes summer meetings are held in the yard, at the home of a member for a picnic or at a park or church large enough to accommodate the families of members. Programs are always interesting. Sometimes local officials, authors or people of note come to discuss topics of current interest. Chapter members present programs on historical subjects and state and national meetings. Each October, the program focuses on the beginning of the chapter and its past accomplishments. In October 1973, for example, an account of the fiftieth anniversary of the chapter was read and pictures shown of earlier times. Nine daughters who had been members for twenty-five years were present, and six members were honored for their fifty years of membership. It was a testimony to the hard work, edification and loyalty of the members. At that meeting, a demonstration of the spinning wheel was given by a member. A display of antique coverlets was shown and discussed at the October 1974 meeting. These had been displayed at the Indiana State DAR Convention and were also on display at the house during the Harvest

Homecoming Open House that year. Participating in the centennial of the Indiana DAR, Piankeshaw Chapter submitted 222 names to be included in the "Roster of Ancestors of Indiana."

Historical essay contests in the schools have been sponsored in most years. Essays are written on topics established by the national organization. The contest brought 313 entries in 1968. Some years a "History Teacher of the Year" has been honored. Many essay winners in our contests have gone on to win at the state and national levels. Other honors include the following: Good Citizenship Awards for eighth-grade students; ROTC awards for high school seniors; and Good Citizen awards, also for high school seniors. Winners, their families and teachers are recognized with a reception at Scribner House.

There were several musicians in the chapter during the 1950s and 1960s, and sometimes others were asked to perform. In 1958 it was announced that the Piankeshaw Chorus would sing at the Sixtieth Continental Congress of the DAR in Washington, D.C. The choir presented a program for one of the chapter meetings that year. At another meeting, a string ensemble played in honor of Lillian Emery, who had presided over the schooling of most of them.

From its early years, the chapter has made the house available to other organizations to hold meetings. Organized tours began when Lillian Emery was an active member. She brought a Girl Scout troop to the house to learn about its history and the history of New Albany. From that time, tours of students, teachers' groups and anyone who wished to schedule tours of the house have been welcomed. Members trained as docents have presented the history of the beginning of the town and of the house, along with explanations of the artifacts and how our ancestors lived. For several decades, tours have been sponsored by the New Albany–Floyd County School System. Busloads of third graders have enthusiastically visited the house. Groups of foreign students have also been welcomed. Open House is held during Harvest Homecoming days and by appointment. A railroad tour from Huntingburg scheduled a stop of several hours in New Albany on June 9–10, 1979. Plans to open the house for that group included an antique wagon display at the rear of the house. Each year, Scribner House participates in the May Walking Tour of Mansion Row, sponsored by the Floyd County Historical Society, by holding an open house at the beginning of the tours. An open house by invitation only was held on December 28, 1986, in appreciation for local businesses and organizations that had supported the Scribner House Fund.

During 1987, the chapter approved the loan of articles from Scribner House for a one-month public exhibit in the New Albany Public Library. The three portraits by George Morrison were loaned to the Culbertson Mansion from June 6 through June 13, 1987, for an exhibit on Morrison. Later on, in February 2006, the Carnegie Center for Art and History requested the loan of the Morrison portraits from Scribner House as part of an exhibit of Morrison paintings. Also in 1987, the organ belonging to Miss Hattie was restored to working order.

In 1988, New Albany celebrated its dodransbicentennial (175th anniversary). The chapter regent, assisted by an American history teacher at Scribner Junior High School, located nearly one hundred Scribner descendants. The 175th anniversary celebration was called Scribner Days and took place on June 17–19, 1988. Many Scribner descendants were in attendance.

In 1988, the chapter celebrated its seventieth anniversary with forty-four members present and twenty members of the Fincastle Chapter from Louisville, Kentucky, as guests. The Fincastle Chapter presented two chairs to the chapter as a gift. Minutes of the first Piankeshaw Chapter meeting from 1898 were read. Lillian Emery was asked to reminisce on chapter events. She spoke of the purchase of the house from the Scribner family; the mortgage being paid off in 1928; the upper floor being restored in 1932; the 1937 flood, which destroyed so much that had taken so long to accomplish; and of the 1960s, when the ladies braided rugs for the house.

Piankeshaw Chapter has always cooperated with the state and national organizations. In 1905, the Indiana State DAR conference was hosted jointly by Piankeshaw Chapter and Anne Rogers Clark Chapter of Clark County. Since that time, Piankeshaw has entertained many meetings of the Southern District DAR Chapters, approximately every six years. Each year in November, Piankeshaw Chapter and Anne Rogers Clark Chapter share a luncheon meeting, alternating as the hostess chapter. These events have been held in various churches or clubs large enough to serve luncheons to the large attendance. Piankeshaw Chapter was also credited with donating approximately seven hundred pages of previously unpublished material to the NSDAR Library in Washington, D.C. It consisted of church records and cemetery listings.

The list of projects to which the chapter has contributed is long. An ongoing focus has been the support of DAR sponsored or approved mission schools—Tammassee School in Tammassee, South Carolina; Kate Duncan Smith School in Grant, Alabama; and Hindman Settlement School in Hindman, Kentucky, were all in special need. Funds as well as many boxes of clothing and supplies were contributed. Preservation and maintenance of our national headquarters, Continental Hall and Constitution Hall in Washington, D.C., receive support yearly. Numerous scholarship funds and the establishment and care of historic monuments have received attention. Many books have been donated to the National DAR library and to hospitals. Gifts were collected to send to Ellis Island for the use of immigrants and their families for many years.

In January 1984, the Children of the American Revolution (C.A.R.) was organized by Piankeshaw Chapter. There were twenty-three charter members plus twenty-two applications sent to the national DAR for approval. This made the Richard Lord Jones C.A.R. Society the second largest in Indiana. Membership in the C.A.R. is available to both boys and girls whose documented proof of their descent from Revolutionary Patriots is accepted by the national society. Members "age out" of C.A.R. on their twenty-second birthday and can use their national C.A.R. number with an application to join either the Daughters of the American Revolution or Sons of the American Revolution. One of the projects accomplished by the local chapter of the C.A.R. was to plant sixteen dogwood trees at Scribner House.

The Southern Indiana District meeting of DAR Chapters was held in New Albany on August 4, 2007. Much planning and hard work by the chapter members made it a very successful and well-attended gathering. State and regional officers, as well as a national officer, were present for the luncheon meeting held at the Graceland Baptist Church social hall.

In 2002, Piankeshaw Chapter was honored by the Indiana State DAR in eleven categories. It won first place in membership with the largest membership percentage increase. The chapter also won a Chapter Achievement Level 1 award for its high level of overall participation in the National DAR.

The DAR chapter hosts two gala events in December each year after Scribner House has been decorated for the season. After the Christmas Tea and open house comes the regular meeting of the chapter, to which guests are specially invited. In 2002, the evening meeting featured a delightful Christmas concert by the Jamie Abersold Jazz Band. This has become an annual event that has continued for its ninth season in 2011. The music is followed by holiday refreshments and an extended social hour.

In June 2010, members of the chapter, along with the Floyd County Historical Society Auxiliary, prepared finger foods to be served at a Develop New Albany fundraiser held at the home of the mayor. The event was repeated in 2011, and money raised was shared with the Floyd County Historical Society and Develop New Albany.

Along with the usual annual activities of the chapter during 2009–10, a project was carried out as part of the Indiana State DAR Project Patriot.

The chapter members personally donated $446 for the presentation of prepaid phone cards for soldiers being deployed from Camp Atterbury.

In order to work in conjunction with the Floyd County Historical Society Padgett Museum, the chapter kept open house on Saturdays through the fall of 2011 and during Harvest Homecoming. At that time, a sales table in the front yard brought in money from the sale of baked goods and items from the gift shop. It also served to make the public more aware of Scribner House.

In recent years members of Piankeshaw Chapter have served the national DAR. In 2011, the chapter was honored when a national DAR Historic Preservation Award was presented to a chapter member, Pamela Peters, for research on the history of the Underground Railroad and its Floyd County connections. The research resulted in a book and a permanent exhibit in the Carnegie Center for Art and History in New Albany.

During 2011–12, a committee was formed to work on compiling a book about the Scribner House through its history covering two centuries. This involved tedious and time-consuming review of chapter minutes since its founding in 1898. The committee extracted information concerning Scribner House and its care and relevant, interesting facts and activities regarding the house, the history of New Albany and the DAR Chapter.

Meanwhile, the tours of Scribner House for schoolchildren and others under the guidance of two or three docents at a time has continued. The annual Historical Essay Contest has been sponsored, the annual Christmas Tea and open house continues to be a social event for New Albany and the chapter continues to host an annual meeting with the Ann Rogers Clark Chapter. Our present regent has the honor of becoming Southern Indiana district director. Monthly meetings continue where members gather to learn from interesting speakers and projects and concerns of the national organization. Always, there is the process of maintaining Scribner House and finding ways to finance its perpetuation.

For 114 years, Piankeshaw Chapter has lived and grown strong in the hearts of its members and deeply respected in the community. With its history preserved for posterity at Scribner House, Piankeshaw Chapter of the DAR, along with help from this community, will continue to face new goals with enthusiasm and contribute generously to the continued preservation of Scribner House and the fulfillment of the objectives of the National Society of the Daughters of the American Revolution. How fortunate we are that goals of the DAR and the preservation of Scribner House fit together so well. It was meant to be!

Chapter 6

A Walking Tour of Scribner House

TOUR INTRODUCTION

Tour groups that visit Scribner House are met by docents who welcome them and tell about the Scribner family and the history of the house. They explain the many artifacts in the house and the care given it by the Daughters of the American Revolution since 1917. In the front yard, guests enter through the rose arbor and gate at the front picket fence. The large old tulip poplar tree, the Indiana state tree, and the peony bushes, the state flower, are noted. The large stone before the front door originally served as the doorstep for the log cabin built by the first settler in Floyd County, Patrick Shields. The brass doorknocker and the nameplate inscribed "W.A. Scribner" are original to the house, as is hardware throughout.

Entering the hallway, the music room is on the left. Here the docents explain that Joel, Nathaniel and Abner Scribner founded New Albany in 1813. They were the sons of Nathaniel Scribner Sr., who was a soldier in the American Revolutionary War. Prior to 1812, Joel, his wife and seven children, along with Joel's sister Phebe; her husband, William Waring; their children, and William Waring's brother Harry, all traveled from New York to Cincinnati via covered wagon and flatboat to start a tannery business there. In 1812, the two Waring brothers left Cincinnati to join the army and fight in the War of 1812. At that time, Joel asked his brothers Nathaniel and Abner to come to Cincinnati to help him. The three brothers made the decision to start a new town. They decided on the area now known as New Albany and

Scribner House at the time of the annual holiday walking tour. *Photo by K. Holwerk.*

purchased the land from John Paul, the founder of Madison, Indiana. The Scribner brothers, who came from the New York City area, named their new town after the capital of their home state of New York, but the Scribners never actually lived in Albany. The Scribner and Waring families lived in a double log cabin on High Street (now Main) until Joel's new home was built. It was made of post and beam construction with unglazed brick used inside the exterior wooden weatherboarding.

In 1814, Joel's family moved to the new home. Scribner House remained in the family until Harriet Rowland Scribner (Miss Hattie) sold the home to Piankeshaw Chapter Daughters of the American Revolution in 1917 for $1,500. It took the DAR eleven years to pay off the mortgage. In 1932, a major restoration took place. Scribner House survived the major flood of 1937, but again, much restoration work needed to be done after the flood.

Scribner House was the first frame house built in New Albany and is the oldest house standing today. It is unique in that only Scribner family members have lived in the house. First was Joel Scribner, his wife and family. He died in 1823. The second owner was William Augustus Scribner, son of Joel, who came to New Albany with his father at the age of thirteen, became a physician and raised his family in the house. He was born in 1800 and died in 1868. The third owner was Harriet Rowland Scribner, daughter of William Augustus, who was born in 1835 and died in 1917 at Scribner House. She was an accomplished music teacher who became quite poor in her later years. She was a member of the DAR to whom she eventually sold the house. It is unique, too, that the house contains so much that belonged to the Scribner family. The house was always a home. Members of Piankeshaw Chapter have lovingly preserved this home. It has been maintained as nearly as possible in the way it looked when the Scribner family lived there. Little has been changed except returning the windows to their original short length, removing the wall between music room and parlor to provide more space for meetings, and adding modern wiring, heating, air conditioning and plumbing. A small, contemporary kitchen and lavatory have been added in the space originally used for firewood under the rear porches.

From time to time, it has been necessary to make repairs, paint or wallpaper the house, but the appearance remains essentially the same. The curtains are similar to what the Scribners used. At one time, the parlors had rose-patterned carpeting, but that long since wore out or was destroyed by floodwaters. Notice the beautiful braided rugs made by the members of the DAR during the 1950s and 1960s. They are made of wool strips cut from used clothing. We are proud of our outstanding collection of textiles, paintings and antiques, many of which belonged to the Scribner family.

MUSIC ROOM

The **rocking chair** with short runners was brought by Joel in 1813 from New York. It rocks fast and is said to make a baby go to sleep faster.

The **desk top** belonged to Charles Edward Scribner, the youngest son of William Augustus Scribner. It was a gift from his parents for his ninth birthday and made in New Orleans. Many of the books in the house also belonged to "Little Eddie."

The **slate** is believed to have belonged to "Little Eddie."

The **cane-bottomed chair** was used by Miss Hattie when she gave piano lessons. It sits low so that she could watch her pupil's fingers move correctly on the piano keys. In her later years, she gave the little chair to one of her students, and the chair was gone for many years. It was given back to the house several years ago by the student's family.

The **pump organ** belonged to Miss Hattie. It has been restored and still plays.

Charles Edward "Little Eddie" Scribner's desk. *Photo by C.W. Branham*, News and Tribune.

Miss Hattie's organ. *Photo by C.W. Branham,* News and Tribune.

Square piano. *Photo by K. Holwerk.*

The **picture of Mount Vernon** belonged to the Scribner family.

The **portrait** above the mantel is of Dr. William Augustus Scribner. The artist is believed to be George Morrison. William kept a diary, and this is how we know so much about the family and the founding of New Albany. The original diary is in our public library. The portrait was restored in 1992 at a cost of over $7,300.

The **pink flowered shawl** on the table belonged to the Scribners. The shawl was probably brought as a gift to Harriet Hale Scribner from New Orleans by her brother, Dr. David Hale. It was returned to the DAR by a Scribner descendant in December 1970.

The **brass candlestick** belonged to Joel and came with him in 1813.

The **sampler** was made in 1824 by six-year-old Charlotte Alsop. Note the beautiful colors that have not faded.

The **antique square piano** was donated by the family of Miss Adelia Woodruff, who was a member of Piankeshaw Chapter DAR. The piano survived the 1937 flood when there was over six feet of water in this room. It was restored in 2004, and the music on the piano belonged to the Scribner family. Miss Hattie had given her square piano to a niece.

The **pictures of George and Martha Washington** over the piano belonged to the Scribners.

BACK PARLOR

This room was used as the schoolroom where Joel's daughter Lucy Marie was the teacher. It was also used as a meetinghouse by the Presbyterians until their church was built. The Scribners were members and founders of the first Presbyterian Church here. When the Scribners sold land, a part of the money received for the sale was set aside for the schools. That money is still in our school system today. Every year, a boy or a girl from the two high schools, New Albany and Floyd Central, receives a scholarship from the interest. The Scribners also gave land for schools and city government buildings. After the dodranscentennial (175th), several Scribner descendants donated hundreds of dollars to supplement this Scribner Fund.

The **Hepplewhite half-moon-shaped banquet table** belonged to Joel and originally had two pieces. This piece had been thrown out of the house and was found on the woodpile when the DAR purchased the house. When it was found, members of the DAR restored it. It is unknown what happened to the other half except that Miss Hattie was very poor and it may have been used for firewood. It was probably brought by Joel in 1813.

The **portrait** above the mantel is of Harriet Partridge Hale, the second wife of Dr. William Augustus Scribner and the mother of Charles Edward Scribner. The artist is George Morrison.

The **picture of Columbus** over the game table belonged to the Scribners.

The **Victorian chair** is said to have belonged to the Scribner family

The **spool table** belonged to Miss Hattie, and she kept her music on it.

The **settee and two matching chairs** were a wedding gift to a granddaughter of Joel Scribner, Mary Scribner David Collins, but they were never used in the house until she gave them to Scribner House. She was a member of Piankeshaw Chapter DAR and also one of our regents.

The **cherry desk** belonged to an early mayor of New Albany, Judge Hooper. It was given to Scribner House by his niece, a member of our chapter.

The **three pictures** on the west wall are originals belonging to the Scribner family. The top picture may be of Miss Hattie, the middle one is "Little Eddie" and the third one is Caroline Scribner, three children of William Augustus Scribner.

The **antique gold floor-to-ceiling mirror** was given to Scribner House through the estate of Elizabeth Payne. Mrs. Payne was a past regent and member of this DAR chapter. Her mother, Margaret Siebolt Johnson, was a charter member of this chapter.

The framed medallion was presented to the chapter by the Neely family in 2003. It was awarded to a member of the Society of the Cincinnati, which was organized after the close of the Revolutionary War to honor the officers of the Continental Line and their French counterparts. George Washington was elected its first president general. It was found during dredging operations in the Ohio River.

The **Christian doors** are original to the house. They were often used in houses of that period and they are till being used today.

The **doorknobs** are agate and are original to the house.

The **portrait** is of Charles Edward Scribner ("Little Eddie"), who was born in 1846 and died in 1879. He is the son of Dr. William Augustus Scribner and his second wife, Harriet Partridge Hale. The artist is George Morrison.

Main-Floor Hall

The **lantern,** now used as a light fixture in the hall ceiling leading to the stairs to the second floor, was a Scribner hand lantern. It was modified for electricity in 1928 when electricity was first put in the house.

Second-Floor Stairwell

The **portrait of Charles Shipman** was given to Scribner House during the celebration of New Albany's dodransbicentennial (175th) in 1988 by a descendant of Nathaniel Scribner, Stewart Webster Purdy Jr. of California. It is a copy of the original in Mr. Purdy's possession. Charles Shipman was the husband of Lucinda Scribner, the only child of Nathaniel Scribner, founder of New Albany. Mr. Purdy told of the matching picture of Lucinda being slashed by vandals trying to get the original, beautiful, oval, gold frame. After her father's death, Lucinda was adopted by Dr. Asahel Clapp, New Albany's first doctor, who married Nathaniel's widow, Elizabeth. Charles Shipman was a prominent shipbuilder here.

FRONT BEDROOM

The **three mourning pieces** are the pictures on the inside, west, north and east walls. They were sent when someone died, just as we send flowers and cards today. The painted one over the table on the east wall is a Scribner piece and was sent to the Scribner family when Dr. Scribner's first wife died. The one on the inside west wall is made of dried leaves and flowers, and the one between the two windows on the north side is needlepoint.

The **shawls** on the two chairs on either side of the table belonged to the Scribner family.

The **table** to the left of the fireplace belonged to Charles Edward Scribner ("Little Eddie").

The **metal hot water bottle** on the mantel belonged to Dr. William Augustus Scribner.

Money scales are on the mantel.

The **wooden cup** on the mantel held powder that was used to sprinkle on letters to help dry the ink.

The **old-fashioned glasses** were hunting glasses from Sears, Roebuck and Co., dating to 1908. Their amber color aided sight during morning fogs.

The **medicine bags** belonged to Dr. Clapp. He boarded at Scribner House and later married Joel's daughter Mary Lucinda, who died in childbirth. Dr. Clapp taught Dr. William Augustus Scribner medicine. Dr. Clapp married a second time to the widow of Nathaniel Scribner and adopted Nathaniel's daughter, Lucinda, as his own.

The **fire screen** was used to protect the ladies' faces from the heat of the fireplace.

The **boot jack** was used to remove boots.

The **saddlebags** were used on the back of a horse to carry provisions.

The **picture** above the fireplace is a later picture of Dr. William Augustus Scribner.

The **clothes** in the closet were in the possession of Miss Hattie Scribner at the time of her death and were found in the house by the DAR when they purchased the house.

The **camelback trunk** belonged to Dr. Scribner and was made in New Albany. Dr. Scribner's initials are on the side.

The **pictures** on the inside wall are of Scribner House in 1850 and Dr. Scribner. Both are original.

BACK BEDROOM

The **glass cabinet** contains many Scribner items: nightcaps, fans, jewelry, Dr. Scribner's tuning fork, under-sleeves, silver curtain tie-backs, Dr. Scribner's coffee and tea service, Miss Hattie's calling card cases, button string and "Little Eddie's" music stand.

The **Hepplewhite bed** is also called a pencil post bed and dates back to 1740. It was given to Scribner House by Albert Hise, a curator of a museum in Ohio, whose grandparents were from New Albany. He also gave the **chest of drawers** and **Chippendale mirror**. The bed has a rope foundation and feather mattress.

The **quilt** at the foot of the bed on the quilt stand belonged to a descendant of Nathaniel Scribner. It was made by the ladies of St. Paul's Episcopal Church in 1870 for Charlotte Shipman Purdy, daughter of Lucinda Scribner Shipman, as a "going away" present when she and her husband, the pastor at St. Paul's, took a new pastoral position in Minneapolis, Minnesota. It was

given to Scribner House during Scribner Days in 1988 by a descendant, Joan Purdy Roney.

The **pictures of George and Martha Washington** over the fireplace belonged to the Scribners.

The **Boston rocker** belonged to the Scribner family.

The **pulley** on the upstairs porch is original and was installed by Joel Scribner when the house was built. It was used to pull or haul things up from the lower level.

Bedroom. *Photo by K. Holwerk.*

Original pulley on upstairs porch, installed by Joel Scribner. *Photo by C.W. Branham,* News and Tribune.

Dr. William Augustus Scribner's **top hat** is on the blanket chest.

The original **picture of Harvey Augustus Scribner** hangs on the south wall. He was the oldest son of Dr. William Augustus Scribner. It was given to Scribner House during Scribner Days in 1988 by Mrs. Clifford Scribner.

Dressing Room

This room was built as a dressing room, but in later years, it was used as a bedroom for "Little Eddie."

The **dress** in the corner dates back to 1830.

The **white dress with pale pink bows** was a wedding dress worn in 1900.

The **brown taffeta dress** was a wedding dress worn in 1900, but the material dates back to 1865.

The **sewing machine** was one of the first in New Albany.

The **mirror** over the sewing machine may have belonged to the Scribners.

The **trunk** was the trousseau trunk of Caroline Matilda Chapman, first wife of Dr. Scribner.

The **white kid shoes** on top of the trunk were worn by "Little Eddie's" wife, Nannie E. Day, on her wedding day.

Nursery on the Top Floor

Lillian Emery, past regent of Piankeshaw Chapter DAR, restored the attic nursery and collected many of the toys in the collection. Two of the **doll beds** belonged to Miss Emery and were made for her by her father. A photograph of Miss Emery hangs in the nursery to honor her efforts to develop the fine collection.

The **bed, chest of drawers and wardrobe** all belonged to the Scribners. The bed originally had a canopy that was removed when the bed was moved to the top floor.

The **cradle** at the foot of the bed has been used by at least four generations.

The **dolls** on the chest of drawers are similar to what Mrs. Scribner would have made for her children. There are an apple head doll, two corn husk dolls and one made of a hickory nut and cloth. These dolls are reproductions. Notice the original "dressmaker" or "French fashion" dolls See the **doll with**

Sewing machine. *Photo by K. Holwerk.*

Third-floor nursery. *Photo by K. Holwerk.*

the metal head. She is wearing a yellow hat and sweater. The **bisque doll with a pink dress** in the white carriage was brought from Germany in the mid-1800s. The **Daisy Blanche doll** belonged to Miss Emery.

The **leather shoes** on top of the shelf over the window can be worn on either foot and were said to have belonged to "Little Eddie."

The **east window well** is where the Scribner girls liked to play. On either side of the window are all of the flues from all of the fireplaces in the house, so it was a warm and cozy spot.

The **two toy black cast-iron stoves** were typical of real stoves of the Victorian period. These stoves were toys or possibly salesman's samples.

(Note: None of the toys belonged to the Scribners.)

Kitchen

This was Mrs. Scribner's kitchen, and we say it was the first family room in New Albany. At one time, the beamed ceiling was exposed. This room was totally underwater during the 1937 flood.

Kitchen fireplace. *Photo by K. Holwerk.*

The pictures on the wall at the foot of the stairs show Scribner House in different years. Note the six-on-six windows in Scribner House in 1850. After that time, Dr. Scribner modernized the house and changed the windows to be of the long style of the Victorian period. In 1932, the DAR changed the windows back to those of the 1850 period. The picture of the Scribner family was taken in front of Scribner House in 1913 during the celebration of New Albany's 100th birthday. The older lady sitting in the middle is Miss Hattie. After Scribner Days in 1988, all of the family members were identified.

The **picture of the Constitutional Elm** (the Hoosier Elm), is the way the tree looked when Indiana's constitution was signed under it in Corydon, Indiana, our first state capital.

The **large spinning wheel** is also called a walking wheel. Only wool can be spun on it.

The **yarn winder or weazel** was used to measure the spun yarn. When it reaches a certain number of feet, it pops, thus the name of the song "Pop Goes the Weasel."

The **large and heavy churn-like object** was Mrs. Scribner's washing machine.

The **blue bowls** on the mantel and the **blue platter and serving bowl** on the folding game table belonged to the Scribners.

The **clock** on the mantel belonged to the Scribners.

The **blue pitcher** on the mantel belonged to the Scribners.

The **iron crane** is original and many of the iron pots in the fireplace belonged to the Scribners.

A **wooden sausage grinder** is in the fireplace.

Notice **the irons and the shoe lasts** in and near the fireplace.

The **smaller spinning wheel** spins either wool or cotton.

The **jelly and jam chest** belonged to the Scribners and survived the 1937 flood.

Notice **the piece of glass and the glass jars** from the New Albany Glass Factory that also produced the first plate glass window in the United States.

Notice the **candle mold and the ruching irons**, for ironing pleats in collars and trim, in the window well.

The **two chairs with woven seats** on either side of the table between the west windows belonged to Dr. Clapp.

The Scribner House has many interesting items not described in this brief tour.

Sketch of Scribner House by Ruth Lenahan. *Courtesy Piankeshaw Chapter DAR.*

Nathaniel and Phebe Scribner Family Tree

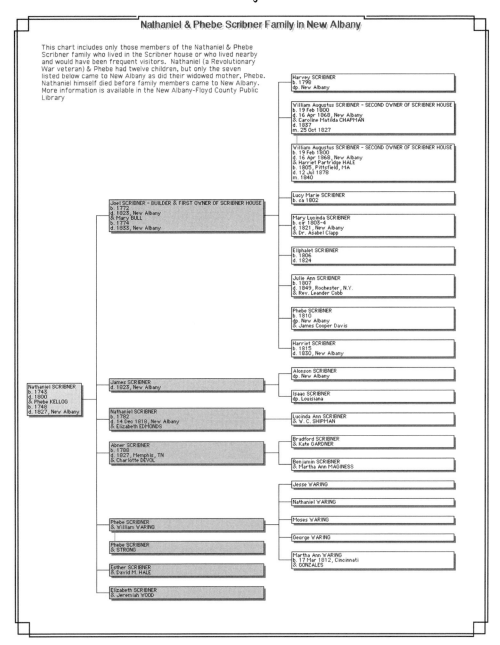

Nathaniel & Phebe Scribner Family in New Albany

This chart includes only those members of the Nathaniel & Phebe Scribner family who lived in the Scribner house or who lived nearby and would have been frequent visitors. Nathaniel (a Revolutionary War veteran) & Phebe had twelve children, but only the seven listed below came to New Albany as did their widowed mother, Phebe. Nathaniel himself died before family members came to New Albany. More information is available in the New Albany-Floyd County Public Library

Nathaniel SCRIBNER
b. 1743
d. 1800
& Phebe KELLOG
b. 1748
d. 1827, New Albany

Joel SCRIBNER – BUILDER & FIRST OWNER OF SCRIBNER HOUSE
b. 1772
d. 1823, New Albany
& Mary BULL
b. 1774
d. 1833, New Albany

- **Harvey SCRIBNER**
  b. 1798
  dp. New Albany

- **William Augustus SCRIBNER – SECOND OWNER OF SCRIBNER HOUSE**
  b. 19 Feb 1800
  d. 16 Apr 1868, New Albany
  & Caroline Matilda CHAPMAN
  d. 1837
  m. 25 Oct 1827

- **William Augustus SCRIBNER – SECOND OWNER OF SCRIBNER HOUSE**
  b. 19 Feb 1800
  d. 16 Apr 1868, New Albany
  & Harriet Partridge HALE
  b. 1805, Pittsfield, MA
  d. 12 Jul 1878
  m. 1840

- **Lucy Marie SCRIBNER**
  b. ca 1802

- **Mary Lucinda SCRIBNER**
  b. cir 1803-4
  d. 1821, New Albany
  & Dr. Asabel Clapp

- **Eliphalet SCRIBNER**
  b. 1806
  d. 1824

- **Julie Ann SCRIBNER**
  b. 1807
  d. 1849, Rochester, N.Y.
  & Rev. Leander Cobb

- **Phebe SCRIBNER**
  b. 1810
  dp. New Albany
  & James Cooper Davis

- **Harriet SCRIBNER**
  b. 1815
  d. 1830, New Albany

James SCRIBNER
d. 1823, New Albany

- **Alonson SCRIBNER**
  dp. New Albany

- **Isaac SCRIBNER**
  dp. Louisiana

Nathaniel SCRIBNER
b. 1782
d. 14 Dec 1818, New Albany
& Elizabeth EDMONDS

- **Lucinda Ann SCRIBNER**
  & W. C. SHIPMAN

Abner SCRIBNER
b. 1788
d. 1827, Memphis, TN
& Charlotte DEVOL

- **Bradford SCRIBNER**
  & Kate GARDNER

- **Benjamin SCRIBNER**
  & Martha Ann MAGINESS

Phebe SCRIBNER
& William WARING

- **Jesse WARING**

- **Nathaniel WARING**

- **Moses WARING**

- **George WARING**

- **Martha Ann WARING**
  b. 17 Mar 1812, Cincinnati
  & GONZALES

Phebe SCRIBNER
& STRONG

Esther SCRIBNER
& David M. HALE

Elizabeth SCRIBNER
& Jeremiah WOOD

Scribner family tree. *Curtis Peters.*

Joel and Mary Scribner Family Tree

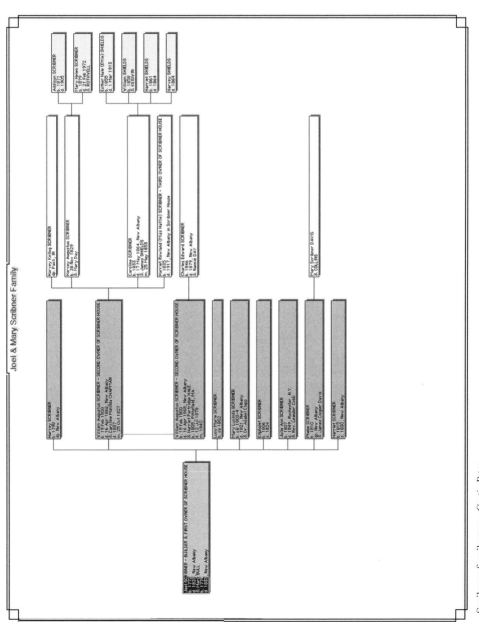

Joel & Mary Scribner Family

Harvey Kellog SCRIBNER
d. Paoli, IN

Addison SCRIBNER
b. 1871
d. 1905

Harvey Augustus SCRIBNER
b. 28 Nov 1829
& Mary Day

Mary Helen SCRIBNER
b. 1879
d. 21 Feb 1972
& ROTHWELL

Harvey SCRIBNER
d. New Albany

Caroline SCRIBNER
b. 1835
d. 17 May 1864, New Albany
& James SHIELDS
m. 25 May 1853

Esther Hale (Ette) SHIELDS
b. 1854
d. 1 Mar 1913

William SHIELDS
b. 1855
& KEDDVIN

Harriet SHIELDS
b. 1861
d. 1864

Harvey SHIELDS
d. 1864

William Augustus SCRIBNER – SECOND OWNER OF SCRIBNER HOUSE
b. 9 Feb 1800
d. 16 Apr 1862, New Albany
& Caroline Matilda CHAPMAN
b. 1807, Pittsfield, MA
m. 25 Oct 1827

Harriet Rowland (Miss Hattie) SCRIBNER – THIRD OWNER OF SCRIBNER HOUSE
b. 1835
d. 1917, New Albany in Scribner House

Charles Edward SCRIBNER
b. 1846
d. 1879, New Albany
& Nannie DAY

William Augustus SCRIBNER – SECOND OWNER OF SCRIBNER HOUSE
b. 16 Apr 1868, New Albany
& Martha Partridge HALE
b. 1825, Pittsfield, MA
m. 2 Jul 1879
m. 1940

Lucy Marie SCRIBNER
b. ca 1802

Mary Lucinda SCRIBNER
b. 1834–4
d. 1821, New Albany
& Dr. Asabel Clapp

Elphalet SCRIBNER
b. 1806
d. 1824

Julie Ann SCRIBNER
b. 1807
d. 1849, Rochester, N.Y.
& Rev. Leander Cobb

Philo SCRIBNER
b. 1810
d. New Albany
& James Cooper Davis

Mary Scribner DAVIS
& COLLINS

Harriet SCRIBNER
b. 1815
d. 1880, New Albany

_____ SCRIBNER – BUILDER & FIRST OWNER OF SCRIBNER HOUSE
b. 1772
New Albany
& _____ BULL
d. 1853, New Albany

List of Piankeshaw Chapter DAR Regents

Miss Mary E. Cardwill 1898–1901
Miss Theodisia E. Hedden 1901–1903
Miss Mary E. Cardwill 1903–1905
Miss Adelia Woodruff 1905–1907
Miss Clara Funk 1907–1909
Mrs. Bella B. Smith 1909–1911
Mrs. Abigail S. Loughmiller 1911–1913
Mrs. Annabellah S. Hartley 1913–1915
Mrs. Margaret M. Sieboldt 1915–1917
Mrs. Elizabeth H. Cannon 1917–1919
Mrs. Mary Scribner Collins 1919–1921
Mrs. Aurelia R. Hickey 1921–1923
Mrs. Caroline R. Stoy McQuiddy 1923–1925
Mrs. Anna W.H. Greene 1925–1927
Mrs. Edna Sagabiel Schrader 1927–1929
Mrs. Pauline Hickey Strack 1929–1931
Miss Lillian Ruth Emery 1931–1933
Mrs. Jessie Baylor Schechter 1933–1934
Miss Mary E. Clark 1934–1936
Mrs. Eleanor Stoy Anderson 1936–1938
Mrs. Fannie Wright Huff 1938–1940
Mrs. Mildred Rogers Hartman 1940–1943

Mrs. Irma Sagabiel Frey 1943–1945
Mrs. Hura Stewart Reisz 1945–1946
Mrs. Ethel Keithley Dickman 1946–1948
Mrs. Verna Sagabiel Babb 1948–1950
Mrs. Hura Stewart Reisz 1950–1951
Mrs. Elizabeth Sieboldt Payne 1951–1953
Miss Carrie Beers 1953–1955
Mrs. Ruth Morris Baker 1955–1957
Mrs. Helen Genung Gordon 1957–1959
Mrs. Virginia Wilson Ehalt 1959–1961
Miss Belle Genung 1961–1963
Mrs. Mary Stoy Mullineaux 1963–1964
Miss Eliza Criswell Fullenlove 1964–1966
Mrs. Mildred Markland Skelly 1966–1968
Mrs. Wynema Rector Wagoner 1968–1970
Mrs. Helen Fullenlove Sherman 1970–1972
Mrs. Hazel Jackson Platt Leist 1972–1974
Mrs. Margaret Keithley Rector 1974–1976
Mrs. Beulah Emery Rhode 1976–1978
Mrs. Margaret Sebree Burgess 1978–1980
Mrs. Dorothy Faulkenburg Hall 1980–1984
Mrs. Wynema Rector Wagoner 1984–1986
Mrs. Elizabeth Brink Bridgwater 1986–1988
Mrs. Virginia Murray Nance 1988–1990
Mrs. Vicky Thresher Zuverink 1990–1992
Mrs. Anna McKim Frederick 1992–1994
Mrs. Betty Sue Hunter 1994–1996
Mrs. Ruth Cotton Bryant 1996
Mrs. Jacqueline McKim Taylor 1996–1997
Mrs. Mary Cuzzort Clipp 1997–1998
Mrs. Vicky Thresher Zuverink,
   Indiana State Regent, 1997–2000
Mrs. Virginia Pattison Hardsaw 1998–2000
Mrs. Joyce Watkins Dreher 2000–2002
Mrs. Alleen Wiggs Scanlon 2002–2004
Mrs. Nona Anderson Bell 2004–2006
Miss Anna McKim 2006–2008
Mrs. Joyce Watkins Dreher 2008–2010
Mrs. Carlene Biggs Price 2010–2012

Appendix IV
"Memories of Scribner House"

Joel Scribner and his family
built me firm and strong
They found a perfect setting
on land where I belong.

They built me on the edge of the forest
where the Piankeshaws lived so long
But soon a town grew around me
With neighbors kind and strong.

The Scribner children
climbed my stairs
and I listened in
on their nightly prayers.

I cherished each room
and windows clear
the children's place
was oh so dear!

They learned to read and cipher
and spin the wheel and sew
Their mama taught them manners
I was proud to watch them grow.

I've been called "old" and "quaint"
simple and neat
I was once the only house
on the street.

Folks seem to like
to hear my stories
about births, weddings
and homestead glories.

So when my doors are open
please come and bring a guest
We'll serve you tea and crumpets
and play music at your request!

—*Alleen Scanlon, 2006*
member, Piankeshaw Chapter DAR

Notes

1. William Augustus Scribner, MD, "Early Days in New Albany: A Personal History With a Short Sketch of the Settlement of New Albany" 1862–67. The original journal is in the possession of the Stuart B. Wrege Indiana History Room, New Albany–Floyd County Public Library.
2. *New Albany Daily Ledger*, 1863.
3. L.A. Williams, *History of the Ohio Falls Cities and Their Counties* vol. 2 (Cleveland: L.A. Williams & Co., 1882), 167.
4. *Columbian Centinel* (Boston, MA), September 11, 1813. Two of these original newspaper advertisements, one from Boston and one from Washington, D.C., are on display in the Floyd County Historical Society Padgett Museum.
5. Williams, *History of Ohio Falls*, 140.
6. D.P. Robbins, MD, *New Albany Ind.: Its Advantages and Surroundings* (New Albany, IN: Ledger Company Printers, June 1892), 22–23.
7. Correspondence of Abner to his wife, Charlotte Devol Scribner, April 25, 1825. Original letters are in the possession of the New Albany–Floyd County Public Library.
8. Letter dated May 22, 1827, from E. Young in Memphis, TN, to Dr. D.M. Hale in New Albany, in possession of the New Albany–Floyd County Public Library.
9. Williams, *History of Ohio Falls*, 140.
10. *Daily Commercial* (New Albany, IN), July 11, 1868. The ad read "Scribner & Maginess, corner of Main & State Sts, Dealers in Drugs Dye Stuffs Patent Medicines Tobacco Perfumery Glass Surgical Instru. & Pure Liquors."

11. Abstract of title to Lot #3 on Upper High Street and the rear one-half of Lot #11 on State Street in Plat #93, City of New Albany, Floyd County, Indiana.
12. Dr. Asahel Clapp diary. The original diary is in the possession of the Indiana State Library, Indianapolis, Indiana. The New Albany–Floyd County Public Library retains a copy.
13. Ibid. See also United States Census Records, Floyd County, 1850.
14. Dr. Asahel Clapp diary.
15. See "Freedom Papers" in Pamela R. Peters, *The Underground Railroad in Floyd County, Indiana* (McFarland & Co., Jefferson, NC, 2001), 137 and 161.
16. *New Albany Daily Ledger*, October 13, 1913.
17. Ibid.
18. Mary Helen Scribner, "The Old House Speaks" (New Albany, IN: Piankeshaw Chapter DAR, date unknown).
19. Mary Helen Scribner Rothwell, "Personalities of Scribner House As I Knew Them" (New Albany, IN: Piankeshaw Chapter DAR, date unknown).
20. Minute Book, Piankeshaw Chapter DAR, New Albany, Indiana, October 15, 1898.
21. Ibid.
22. Gwynne Tuell Potts and Samuel W. Thomas, *George Rogers Clark Military Leader in the Pioneer West & Locust Grove the Croghan Homestead Honoring Him* (Louiseville, KY: Historic Locust Grove, Inc., 2006), 79–80.
23. Minute Book, Piankeshaw Chapter DAR.
24. "First Hand Knowledge," *New Albany Tribune*, May 4, 2003, William Ferguson interview.

About the Authors

Anne Frye Caudill is the widow of the important author Harry M. Caudill, who has written such works as *Night Comes to the Cumberland* about the devastation brought on the Appalachian Plateau. Anne worked with him on the manuscripts and supervised the publication of the more recent editions.

Otis Amanda Dick is the author of *Corydon, Indiana*, published in the Images of America series by Acadia Publishing. She is a first person reenactor and takes the part of Hattie Scribner, Lucy Clark Croghan at Locust Grove, Louisville, KY, as well as other characters. Mandy works at the Falls of the Ohio State Park in Clarksville, Indiana.

Pamela R. Peters is the author of *The Underground Railroad in Floyd County, Indiana*, published by McFarland & Co. She is a member of the Floyd County Historical Society and a board member of several not-for-profit organizations.

Carlene Biggs Price is past southern district director of the DAR and is currently state librarian of the DAR, as well as regent of Piankeshaw Chapter DAR.

All four women are members of Piankeshaw Chapter Daughters of the American Revolution.

Visit us at
www.historypress.net